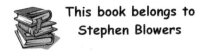

profes
persp

Series Euitoi ...

CW00530334

Spontaneous
Speaking

Drama activities for confidence and fluency

David Heathfield

DELTA
PUBLISHING

Published by
DELTA PUBLISHING
39 Alexandra Road
Addlestone
Surrey KT15 2PQ

© David Heathfield 2005

First published 2005

ISBN 1 900783 92 4

Edited by Helena Gomm
Designed by Christine Cox
Cover illustration by Phillip Burrows
Project managed by Chris Hartley
Printed by Halstan & Co. Ltd., Amersham, Buckinghamshire

Author's acknowledgements

This book is for Mum and Dad.

I'd like to thank:
All the students and teachers who have used these activities and given
invaluable feedback; Richard Tomlinson and all the staff at the Isca School of
English for dedicating time and energy to developing new courses; Peter
Hamilton, theatre director and friend, for inspiring me with drama and so
many great ideas; Tammy, for always making time to listen, suggest, play and
teach and for supporting me, her husband, through times of change; Tom and
Sam for putting up with Dad monopolising the computer; all the writers of ELT
and drama resource books who have provided so much stimulus and whose
ideas have informed mine; Mario Rinvolucri for taking notice and for his
generosity of spirit; Mike Burghall for always being a click away and guiding
me with humour and humanity through the writing process; Helena Gomm for
her perceptive editing and fine-tuning; DELTA Publishing for saying *yes*.

Foreword

Students who participate fully in the classroom, as well as those who find it hard to join in, get a sense of freedom when, for the whole or part of a lesson, they can put aside desks and pens and interact socially, face to face.

My students' stories

A student was chatting away to me at a party one evening. The next day I had my first class with her and I began to understand why a couple of my teaching colleagues had said she didn't participate fully in speaking activities in class. I realised that she, like so many other students I teach, finds it hard to shake off patterns of behaviour she associates with classroom learning. At a social event she felt free to express herself, but, sitting at a table with a book open in front of her and a pen in her hand, she lapsed into unproductive learning habits.

Another, very different student, who was genuinely shy and sensitive in social situations, was used to spending a lot of time observing other people and things which happened around him. When doing the sort of activities described in this book, he always had a great deal to contribute when it came to stepping into a role or describing personal experiences in depth.

My story

After studying for my degree in French and German, I started teaching English in Spain. Spanish came to me in a very different way from my previous formal academic experiences; in fact I learnt mostly through socialising. With the encouragement of my many warm and supportive Spanish friends and students, I found myself acting as if I could speak Spanish even when my vocabulary was still very limited. They gave me the confidence to try out new items of language as I picked them up. I found this a liberating and fun-filled experience.

Returning to the UK, I continued in ELT and discovered a brand new passion for drama with a local theatre group. The more confident I became with drama, the more I started to bring ideas from workshops into the English classroom. I soon realised what an effective tool drama can be for unlocking English skills that students may not realise they already have.

Speaking spontaneously

The activities in this book are for all of us, both the *talkers* and the *listeners*, and they will promote positive classroom dynamics, build confidence and lead to improved fluency. They are activities that I enjoy doing with friends, strangers, fellow actors, fellow teachers and especially with fellow learners. I hope you enjoy them too.

David Heathfield

Contents

Section 3: Personalised Drama Activities 65

Section 4: Conversation Skills 87

Introduction

This book is called *Spontaneous Speaking: Drama activities for confidence and fluency* because that's what it's about. Every activity has been devised, tried out and modified in order to maximise student interaction, using a wide range of language in many different situations which are true-to-life or within the participants' sphere of experience.

Students and teachers alike can benefit a great deal from coming together and learning about each other in a creative and playful way, while at the same time improving their English.

Benefits for the student

- Doing these activities, students have no option but to *speak* and *listen* to each other. Every activity involves extended speaking on the part of every participant, mostly in pair- and groupwork.

- As well as language, students' bodies, minds, emotions and interpersonal skills are involved.

- Students develop their ability to be more spontaneous, fluent and confident in English interaction.

- The activities provide frameworks, but creative content always comes from the students, which leads to a sense of achievement.

- The activities generate a lot of energy, fun and laughter.

- Students can experiment with using language items they are learning in a safe yet true-to-life environment.

- Written prompts such as rolecards are not used, so the students' focus is always 100 per cent on each other.

- The fact that each class member has a purposeful, non-threatening, achievable, extended speaking task to carry out in every activity leads students to remark in feedback how much more they speak than in most classroom speaking activities.

Benefits for the teacher

This book is for you if …

- you want new ideas about how to get your students interacting freely.

- you like simply-explained activities with clear aims and some suggested variations.

- you want to find out how successfully your students can put recently-learnt language into practice.

- you sense your students would benefit from finding out a lot more about each other.

- you want to supplement 'pen, paper, book and desk' work with paper-free activities.

- you want to minimise your input and maximise your students' output.

- you want more fun and laughter in your lessons.

If you teach languages other than English, all the activities in this book would work just as well in your classroom with no extra preparation, with the exception of activities from the Conversation Skills section, which would need a little research.

Activity types

This book is full of activities that involve students in speaking and listening to each other. These activities divide easily into four sections: *Warmers, Drama Activities, Personalised Drama Activities* and *Conversation Skills*. These sections are then subdivided as described on the section introduction pages through the book.

Section 1: Warmers

These activities can be used to bring students together, get them talking and listening to each other and to raise energy levels.

Section 2: Drama Activities

These involve creative extended speaking. Because the content is non-threatening, students shake off their inhibitions and, at the end of an activity, are often surprised at how imaginative they have been.

Section 3: Personalised Drama Activities

These provide a wonderful opportunity for class members not just to talk about their ideas and experiences but to bring them to life in the classroom and really get involved in each other's stories.

Section 4: Conversation Skills

These activities give students the opportunity to explore how native speakers of English interact in everyday conversation through true-to-life drama activities.

Using the activities

You can use one activity as part of a lesson or you can combine two or more to make a complete fluency lesson. Depending on your teaching situation, you might have a regular fluency slot or you might want to build a fluency activity into every lesson.

Levels

The activities are suited to students at a range of levels, partly because of the absence of written prompts. Depending on their level, you may expect different students to be using different vocabulary, expressions and structures.

Time

The timings given in this book are simply guidelines to help you with your planning. The activities will last for different lengths of time with different kinds of groups on different days. However, set time limits, even if you don't stick to them rigidly, are an integral part of the framework and give you and your students more structure within which to be creative.

Language Links

Most of the activities involve students using certain structures, functional language and lexical fields as referred to in Language Links.

- The activities can be used *before* presenting language to diagnose students' needs.

- They can be used for review purposes to find out how successfully students activate language *after* studying and practising it.

- In many cases the same activity can be used *before* and *after* the language points are studied so that students can themselves assess how much progress they have made.

Aims

The main aim is to build confidence, fluency and spontaneity. This comes before the purely linguistic objectives because it is fundamental. Without confidence, learners' progress will be limited. Without spontaneity, interaction will feel less natural. Without either of these, fluency will take longer to achieve.

Class size

The activities suit classes of varying sizes. I have indicated in the teaching notes a minimum or maximum number of participants for the few activities where you need more than four (this can be three students and teacher) or fewer than 40.

Class age

All the activities are suitable for adult and teenage learners, although for the latter group you may sometimes want to opt for the variation I have suggested, as, for example, in *Role Reversals*. Many of the activities have proved hugely successful with young learners, too: the choice will depend on your class.

Mixed-ability classes

The activities suit mixed-level teaching, the emphasis being on fluency. I often find that a student who appears to be at a lower level in terms of accuracy and range of passive vocabulary can be as effective at communicating in English as a higher-level student. This is largely to do with confidence and conversation skills. But even where there are obvious differences, putting levels together can be good for all participants' confidence. Less confident speakers find positive role models, while the more self-assured can get a boost from sometimes giving support to those who need it. In a school where students are streamed according to ability, here is an opportunity to unite students across levels.

Monolingual classes

When teaching monolingual classes, one challenge is always to create an environment where students feel comfortable and confident about speaking English. However, in many classes the students' mother tongue will play an important role. When a student is searching for a particular word or expression, the most natural thing in the world is for them to use their mother tongue or ask a classmate for a quick translation. As their teacher, set yourself achievable goals. If at first students get support from using their mother tongue in the early stages of an activity before doing it again in English, this will be a step in the right direction towards building confidence.

Multilingual classes

Multilingual classes will benefit enormously from using these activities. Students will gain insight into each other's cultures and points of view, and prejudices and barriers may well get broken down. Activities in the *Conversation Skills* section, for example, may lead to discussion about intercultural similarities and differences.

Repetition

All the activities are suitable for repetition by the same students because in every case it is the students themselves who are responsible for the creative content. In fact, some activities lend themselves to frequent and regular repetition and can easily become favourite requests from students.

Materials

On a few occasions some materials are needed, as described at the start of the activity. This might be a piece of music, some photos or even dice or coins, and these will need to be assembled in advance.

'Hands-free' speaking

Normally, no materials are needed at all. It may be tempting for you to provide written prompts for many of these activities, and of course you are free to adapt them as you wish. But bear in mind that holding rolecards and 'useful expressions' prompts can detract from the face-to-face spontaneity of the interaction. If you *do* choose to input language, consider asking students to memorise and practise the pronunciation of the items they need and to put written prompts away *before* they start speaking so that communication is as natural and spontaneous as possible. They can then refer to the prompts again *afterwards* for self-assessment.

Rapport

For positive learning to take place in a classroom, a good teacher–student relationship is of paramount importance. These activities may seem challenging or even risky for some teachers at first, but the benefits will soon become evident. Students will become even more interested in you as a person and will trust you, and be willing to allow you the time and space to lead or demonstrate an activity.

Organising the students

Initially, some students may not be used to this kind of freedom in the language classroom, so tight classroom management is required. The running of activities requires very clear instruction-giving and time-management skills. Your lively input in the role of facilitator is essential for the activities to work.

There are many ways of pairing or grouping students. Avoid allowing students always to work with the same people as this can lead to poor dynamics. I often say 'Stand with someone that you haven't talked to recently'. This means they still have some choice, but don't feel obliged to work with someone they feel less comfortable around. However, there is nothing like drama for overcoming these kinds of inhibitions.

Always be sensitive to those students who feel less confident or need to be included more. You can subtly manage groupings and sometimes work with them yourself. If a student wishes to sit out and observe, they may learn a great deal from the experience. However, this should be the exception rather than the rule as most students start to overcome inhibitions only when they start to involve themselves.

While preparing, try to visualise the activities, i.e. where students are sitting, standing or moving at each stage. I often talk about a starting picture, a frozen image, a photo or a tableau. This means asking students in their pair or group to imagine themselves in a particular location as different characters making a still image which tells us about their attitudes and their relationships. It is an ideal way of making a clear start or end to a dramatised scene. When groups or pairs are going to show their scenes, ask them to make sure that in their still image they are facing the watching students and remind them not to turn their backs. The still image is powerful and fascinating to look at. Counting down '3-2-1 Action' gives both the acting and the watching students a few moments to prepare for the scene. At their final 'showing' stage, many of the activities include a listening task for the watching students. This involves them in the scene and prevents them from preparing for their turn rather than concentrating. A listening, focused audience is essential.

If the activity requires pairs or threes and the class doesn't divide up neatly, consider taking part yourself. Students generally respond positively to their teacher getting involved. Otherwise split roles or have a student sitting out and observing in order to give feedback at the end.

I have used variations of many of these activities in one-to-one teaching. They are ideal for changing the dynamic and bringing 'other characters' into the classroom.

Finally, and this is important, before an activity, briefly explain the aims. At the end, refer students to the aims and invite comments.

Organising the classroom

Students stand up and need to move around in the course of many of these activities. Sometimes the space at the front of the classroom will be enough, but if the students need to form a standing or seated circle, it is advisable to ask them to move tables or desks quickly and quietly to the side.

If you are planning to do a whole lesson of drama activities, ask the students to help you prepare the room as they come in and allow a couple of minutes at the end to transform the space back into a classroom.

Feedback

I would welcome any feedback.
My website is: www.davidheathfield.co.uk;
e-mail address: david@davidheathfield.co.uk.

Further reading

The following have been a source of inspiration for many activities in this book:
Davis, P and Rinvolucri, M *The Confidence Book* Longman 1990
Hargie, O et al *A Handbook of Communication Skills* Croom Helm Ltd 1986
Johnstone, K *Impro: Improvisation and the Theatre* Methuen 1981
Morgan, J and Rinvolucri, M *The Q Book* Longman 1988
Scher, A and Verrall, C *100+ Ideas for Drama* Heinemann 1975

The following contain different types of drama activities from the ones I have concentrated on in this book, but you may find them a good source of inspiration for further drama work:
Chaplin, A *Ideas for Drama KS1* Scholastic 2001
Chaplin, A *Ideas for Drama KS2* Scholastic 2001
Hadfield, J *Classroom Dynamics* OUP 1992
Maley, A and Duff, A *Drama Techniques in Language Teaching* CUP 1980
Phillips, S *Young Learners* OUP 1993
Phillips, S *Drama with Children* OUP 1999
Poulter, C *Playing the Game* Macmillan 1987
Rinvolucri, M *Humanising Your Coursebook* DELTA Publishing 2002
Ross, A, Fulford, J, Hutchings, M and Schmitz, H *Drama* (Bright Ideas Series) Scholastic 1990
Wessels, C *Drama* OUP 1987

1

Warmers

These lively activities get the students involved, energised and thinking. They suit students across the range of levels, mark a definite starting point to a lesson and bring the whole class together.

- The *Greetings* activity can be used as a one-off introduction exercise or every time new members join the class.

- *Mirroring* activities focus students on active listening and remembering.

- *Questions* activities set students fun mental challenges while they learn about each other.

Getting to Know Me

Level

Elementary to Advanced

Time

10 minutes

Language Links

Expressing likes

Aim

To learn and remember other students' names and likes

Variation

You can do this with lots of different likes, e.g. favourite month, food, drink, person, actor, singer, city, animal, etc.

NOTE: You can do the same activity with a different favourite item each week, or every time a new member joins the class as a ritual introduction and a way of making sure everyone knows everyone else's name without any embarrassment.

1 Form a standing circle. Model the procedure first by approaching a few students, saying 'I'm (NAME) and my favourite hobby is … because …' Give the same information each time.

2 Give the students three or four minutes to circulate and to learn or make sure they know everyone's name, hobby and why they enjoy it.

3 Reform the circle. Introduce a student from the other side of the circle by saying 'She's (NAME) and her hobby is …'

4 The named student then introduces another class member and the process continues until the last student introduces you, the teacher.

Mirrors

Level

Elementary to Advanced

Time

10 minutes

Language Links

Sequencing past actions

Aim

To focus on active listening and recount a
sequence of actions

1 Ask the students to face each other in pairs,
A and B.

Model the procedure by telling the students about
how you started the day. For example, 'I woke up
at 7a.m. and looked at my alarm clock. I stayed
in bed for ten minutes then I got up and went to
the bathroom …' Now ask A to do the same.

2 After two minutes, stop A and ask B to repeat
exactly what A said, e.g. 'I woke up at …'

3 Now ask B to recount a detailed sequence of
events, e.g. what he or she did after school
finished the day before.

4 After two minutes, ask A to 'mirror' B's account.

5 Have a class discussion about how easy it is to
remember what your partner has said when you
are listening *actively*, but how most of the time,
even in our own native tongue, we listen
passively. Emphasise that while studying a foreign
language learners need to listen actively a lot
more of the time.

Variations

1 After you have modelled the activity, A recounts,
in detail, what he or she did before the lesson in
reverse order, beginning each sentence, 'Before
that …'. For example, 'Before the lesson I had a
coffee in the canteen with Naoko and before that
I …'. B then repeats back what A said, but now in
chronological order, using 'after that', 'next',
'then', etc.

2 Take a topic which the students have studied
recently and ask them to activate newly learnt
vocabulary. For example, ask them to take turns
to describe their bedrooms – the furniture and the
other objects in them – and to tell their partner
how they feel about them. A and B will remember
and use different items and will prompt and learn
from each other.

Listen and Remember

Level

Lower-intermediate to Advanced

Time

15–20 minutes

Language Links

Past narrative tenses

Aim

To focus on active listening and remembering

1 Form a standing circle. Ask the students to listen very carefully. Give a true two-minute account of how you got here today. Include details, e.g. 'I noticed the daffodils were out.'

2 Put the students in pairs, A and B, and ask them to recall as much as possible of what you said.

3 Ask B to give a detailed two-minute account of how *they* got here today and tell A to listen and remember as much of their partner's account as they can.

4 Ask the students to circulate and tell the As to find new Bs. Ask the As to recount their previous B-partner's journey as accurately as possible without giving away his or her identity.

5 Ask the As to find new Bs again. The Bs then recount what they have just heard of the original B's journey as accurately as possible to their new A-partner.

6 Ask the As to try to find as quickly as possible the original Bs whose journeys they have just heard about, using details to form questions, e.g. 'Did you catch a bus at 8 o'clock?' Once all the pairs are matched, the As recount the journey to the original B who listens and, at the end, comments on how much it has altered.

7 Invite comments and feedback from the whole class.

NOTE: The topic of this activity can be anything. For example, if the students are studying health and fitness vocabulary, they could be asked to talk about what they do to stay healthy.

Yes/No Questions

to Advanced

Time
10 minutes

Language Links
Closed questions

Aim
To practise a variety of possible answers to closed questions

1 Tell the students to ask you as many closed questions as they can. Try to respond without saying 'yes' or 'no'. If you use either of these words, they win the game. As they ask their questions, use a variety of other affirmative and negative responses. After a minute (or when you're caught out), elicit and write on the board as many alternatives to 'yes' and 'no' as possible. For example:

Yes	*No*
that's right	not really
that's true	that's not true
(I'm) sure	surely not
absolutely	absolutely not
definitely	definitely not
you're right	I don't think so
I think so	I'm afraid not
I'd like to	

2 Students play in groups of four to seven. Encourage them to try to catch out the player with trick questions, such as 'Ready?' 'Are you sure?' 'Yesterday?' etc. The winner is the student who avoids saying 'yes' or 'no' for a timed minute *without pausing to answer*!

3 As the groups finish, find out who thinks they did really well. Challenge one of these super-confident people to play in front of the whole class at double speed.

When No Means Yes

Level
> Elementary to Advanced

Time
> 10–15 minutes

Language Links
> Closed questions

Aim
> To practise asking and responding to
> closed questions

1 Ask all the students to think of a question to ask
you which has a 'yes' or 'no' answer. When they
are ready, tell them to fire the questions at you
quickly and in any order. Respond immediately,
trying to say 'yes' when the answer is 'no', and
vice versa. Even if they don't know you well,
they'll soon realise that your answers sometimes
seem a bit strange, e.g. 'Do you like teaching us?'
'No.'

2 Once the students have got the idea (you may
have surprised them in the process!), ask them to
play in groups of four to seven, each taking a turn
at being questioned. Students will usually choose
to ask questions to which they already know the
answer, e.g. 'Are you from another planet?' If
someone manages to give the opposite answer
without hesitating to every question for a timed
minute, they win. The others try to catch them
out by asking tricky questions, e.g. 'Is this an easy
game?' Students learn a surprising amount about
each other's lives and personalities playing this
game.

3 Invite the best player to play again in front of the
whole class, this time at double speed.

Time

10 minutes

Language Links

Personal information questions

Aim

To practise rapid questions and answers

1 Ask each student to think of at least two questions to ask you. Invite the class members to ask you their questions one at a time in quick succession, leaving little time for an answer. Always answer the penultimate question. For example:

'How many children have you got?'
(*don't answer*)
'What's your hobby?'
'Two boys.'
'Do you live near the city centre?'
'Theatre acting.'
'Have you ever eaten *sushi*?'
'Not really, about twenty minutes' walk away.'
'Are you tired?'
'I think I have.'

2 When the students have got the idea, tell them to play the same game in groups of four to six. Encourage the interrogators to ask similar tricky questions in quick succession, e.g. 'How many times have you been to (England?)' 'Have you been to (England) twice?' 'So, when do you think you'll go there again?' etc. The winner is the student who keeps going the longest!

Level

Elementary to Advanced

Time

15–20 minutes

Materials

Three times as many mixed-value coins of the same currency as there are students

Language Links

Personal information questions

Aim

To set a multi-tasking challenge

Variation

Cut out a number of large up-to-date newspaper photos and tear each one into eight. Give each student a turn trying to reassemble one photo while answering questions about how they keep up with the news. This works well as a lead-in to a news lesson.

1 Take a handful of change from your pocket or bag. Tell the students to try to stop you from counting the total amount of money in one minute by asking you as many personal information questions as possible, which you must answer. With higher-level classes, you could theme the questions, e.g. you and money. Point out that open questions are more effective than yes/no questions. If after one minute you cannot give the correct total, your students have won.

2 Tell the students to play the game in groups of four to six. Make sure each player takes a handful of up to 15 mixed-value coins, either their own or provided by you.

3 (Optional) Challenge the most successful student(s) to play again with the whole class asking questions. This time they have to sort the coins according to date (they will need a flat surface for this).

Blind Descriptions

Level
Lower-intermediate to Advanced

Time
10 minutes

Language Links
Question tags

Aim
To practise questions and question tags

1 Ask the students to stand back-to-back in pairs, A and B. Say:

'A, look straight ahead and think about what B is wearing. Ask questions to check if you're right. For example: "You're wearing blue socks, aren't you?" B, ask for further details. For example: "Yes, I'm wearing blue socks, but how long are they, what are they made of and are they dark or light blue?" You've got three minutes to get a detailed description of exactly what B is wearing.'

2 After three minutes, tell A to look at B and check.

3 Blindfold the Bs or ask them to close their eyes. Tell them to think about the room they're in and get ready to describe it. Take the As aside and tell them secretly to encourage B's mistakes by asking for further details but to dismiss correct guesses. For example:

B: I think the wallpaper is green.
A: Right. What shade of green? (It is, in fact, white.)
B: There are three big windows, aren't there?
A: No, not three. (In fact, there are three.)

The Bs will expect their task to be the same as the As' task in stage 1. This will make them susceptible to being conned.

4 After three minutes of being misled by their A partners, let the Bs open their eyes and invite them to comment on how they feel about being duped.

19

2

Drama Activities

In this section, students can be creative while remaining within the framework set by the activity. The activities are sometimes close to students' own lives, but even where the content appears to require a little more fantasy, the structure of the activity gives ample support.

- *Quick-change Roleplay* activities involve the students changing roles and often partners at least twice (and frequently several times!) in quick succession. This is much easier than it sounds and generates energy and positive dynamics. It also enables students to explore situations from different perspectives.

- *Extended Roleplay* activities have students remaining in one role (or sometimes changing once) in the course of the activity. They can explore an issue or situation in more depth and detail and often find themselves expressing their character's feelings.

- *Dramatising Photos* activities involve using visual prompts to enter roles and situations. They also require careful listening on the part of the observing students.

- *Storytelling* is a skill which we don't all realise we have. Through these activities, students realise that, together, they can spontaneously create imaginative and vivid narratives.

- The *Visualisation* activity is simple but revealing. Students learn a lot about one another through a simple question and answer process.

Quick Pairs

Level
Elementary to Advanced

Time
10 minutes

Language Links
Advice and giving instructions

Aim
To manage three dialogues simultaneously

Variation
Use other pairings which give a clear framework but leave scope for imagination and creativity, e.g. violin teacher and student, tour guide and tourist, hairdresser and customer.

1 Put the students in pairs. Tell them all that they are PAIR ONE and ask them to decide who is a *doctor* and who is a *patient*. Then tell them to form different pairs, PAIR TWO, and to decide who is an *actor* and who is a *film director*. Finally, tell them to make new pairs, PAIR THREE, and to be a *ski instructor* and a *beginner skier*.

2 Tell the students that when you call out 'One', they should get together with 'partner one' and start a dialogue and that as soon as you call out a different number they should break off, move to the appropriate partner and start that dialogue. When they meet up with a partner for a second or third time, they continue the dialogue from where they left off.

3 Start off the game, allowing approximately 45 seconds before changing the number. The period of time allowed should vary but should get progressively shorter until the students are 'running'. On the fourth turn of each dialogue, let them know that they should bring that scene to an end in 30 seconds.

Making Friends, Breaking Friends

Level
Elementary to Advanced

Time
10 minutes

Language Links
Starting conversations

Aim
To practise starting and ending social relationships

1 Ask the students to stand in pairs. Say:

'You are two people (not yourselves) and you don't know each other. Talk to each other for one minute and make friends. 3–2–1 Action.'

2 After a minute, say:

'Find a new partner. You're two different people. You know each other very well, but you are having an argument which will end your friendship. 3–2–1 Action.'

3 Get the students to repeat stages 1 and 2 a couple more times, always with a new partner. Remind them each time to be a different person. This should help to make each conversation unique.

Borrowing Neighbours

Level

Elementary to Advanced

Time

10–15 minutes

Language Links

Polite requests and apologies

Aim

To give students confidence in making requests and refusing

1 Put the students in pairs, A and B, asking them to work with a partner they don't know well. Tell them the As have recently moved to a new neighbourhood and that they need to borrow something (not food or drink, but something which they would return) from a neighbour they have never spoken to before. B wants to help but should explain politely why he or she can't. Remind them that the conversation will start off with greetings and friendly introductions. Ask them to mime knocking at the front door.

2 Tell the Bs to stay where they are while each A goes to another B's door, knocks and asks to borrow the same thing(s) as before. This time tell the Bs that they *could* help but don't want to.

3 Send each A to another B who, this time, is pleased to help. They should arrange the return of the item.

4 Tell the students that there has been some kind of problem with the thing(s) A borrowed from their last partner. They should go back and explain. The Bs can respond as they wish.

NOTE: This last stage may give rise to some humour, and some pairs may be happy to explain to the whole class how their problem was or wasn't resolved or even act out the last scene.

Variation

Tell the students that they are going to a party and want to borrow a really special item of clothing they've seen their good friend wearing. It should be a different item from each of the three friends. This is good for reviewing clothes descriptions and words like 'stained', 'torn' and 'scorched'!

Helpful/Unhelpful

Level
Lower-intermediate to Advanced

Time
20 minutes

Materials
Dance music

Language Links
Requests

Aim
To practise making requests and responding helpfully and unhelpfully

NOTE: A minimum of six students is needed for this activity.

1 Put on some dance music (not too loud) and tell the students they are in a nightclub. Tell them they are going to ask for something from someone they don't know, e.g. a barperson, a bouncer, the DJ or another clubber. So that you can model the activity, invite a volunteer to come up and ask you their question. Politely ask them to speak up because of the music (so that everyone can hear). Respond very helpfully in the role they've given you, going out of your way to do all you can to help. Then invite a second volunteer to ask you for something. Say 'What?' and, after hearing the request a second time, be unhelpful *without* being rude, e.g. 'Yeah, just over there near the back.' Don't make too much of the helpful/unhelpful distinction at this stage. Respond to more people's requests, some helpfully, some unhelpfully.

2 Divide the class into As and Bs and ask them to stand on either side of the room. Tell the As that they are on the beach and are going to ask different Bs for different things and to start thinking about their questions. Divide the Bs into two groups, 'helpful' and 'unhelpful', without the As hearing (the music will make this possible). Tell them they'll have to work out their new role each time the As ask for something.

3 Now turn off the music, show the students the beach and where the shoreline is and count down '3–2–1 Action'. After several minutes, bring the scene to an end. Ask the As to group the Bs according to their responses and elicit the labels 'helpful' and 'unhelpful'.

4 Tell the students they are now in a school. Split the As and Bs and put the music on again for a minute so they can't hear your instructions to the other group. Tell *all* the As to be helpful to their first B-partner, unhelpful to the second and so on. After five minutes, ask the Bs to divide the As into groups. This should generate discussion as the Bs will disagree about who is helpful and unhelpful.

Variation

In a Business English class, use appropriate settings, e.g. a company reception area, an international conference, a business lounge at the airport.

Queue-jumping Race

NOTE: If you have fewer than eight participants, make just one queue and time how long it takes each student in turn to get to the front. The next student at the back can start before the previous one arrives at the front. The fastest of all wins.

Level
> Elementary to Advanced

Time
> 15–20 minutes

Language Links
> Persuading

Aim
> To practise persuading people to allow you to jump the queue

1 Form a standing circle. Elicit types of queue and write up a list to include: bus, cinema, outside new art exhibition, railway ticket office, supermarket checkout, first day of sales.

2 Tell the students to form equal length queues (maximum six per queue) down the room. Explain that they are all strangers who want to talk to the people in front and behind them about why they are queuing. The student at the back has to get to the head of the queue by explaining why they should go in front of the next person ahead, who must be persuaded but not too easily.

3 Announce the queue type and start the race. The first student to reach the front of his or her queue wins.

4 Announce a new queue type and tell the new 'back' person to start.

Prized Possessions Swap

Level
Elementary to Advanced

Time
15 minutes

Language Links
Describing objects

Aim
To listen actively and describe objects creatively

1 Ask the students to stand in a circle. Mime picking up and holding an imaginary object of great sentimental value (e.g. your grandmother's watch, a lion's tooth you found in Africa, etc.) and describe it in detail, using the questions in stage 2 below as a prompt. Make it clear from the extraordinariness of your description that the object is not real.

2 Tell the students to mime holding an imaginary object. Ask them to think about their answers to the following questions:

- What is it?
- What does it look like?
- What is it made of?
- Where does it come from?
- How did you get it?
- Why is it special to you?
- Where do you keep it?
- What do you do with it?

3 Tell them to describe their objects to each other in pairs.

4 After the pairs have finished, ask if they would like to swap, explaining that now they can mingle, describing the object they have to each other and at the end choosing whether or not to swap. Make sure that if they *do* swap, they then describe their newly acquired possession to their next partner.

5 After about ten minutes, stop the class and ask some or all of the students to describe the object they have now got and what they're going to do with it. It may be amusing to find how much objects have changed.

Variation

After you have given your description, ask the students either to describe an imaginary object or to describe an extraordinary object they really own which the others don't know about (but without letting the others know whether it is real or not). At the end of the game, they can enjoy guessing whose possessions are real.

Bad Day, Good Day

Level
Elementary to Advanced

Time
30–35 minutes

Language Links
Offers and refusals

Aim
To practise expressing positive and negative feelings in everyday situations

1 Elicit from the students and write up a list of six people going about their work who they might talk to on a typical day, starting in the morning. Depending on where you teach, this might be a variation on the following list:

- newsagent
- bus driver
- supermarket shelf-stacker
- barperson
- someone in a cinema box office
- taxi driver

2 Tell the students to form an outer circle and an inner circle of equal numbers, facing each other in pairs. If necessary, join in to make an even number. Say to the inner circle:

'You are students and you had a really bad day yesterday. It all started early in the morning when you went to the newsagent's.'

The students spontaneously roleplay the encounter, with their outer circle partner as the newsagent.

3 After about 90 seconds, stop the students and move the inner circle clockwise one place, saying:

'The morning continued badly when you got on the bus.'

The outer circle are now all bus drivers.

4 Repeat the process until all six encounters are complete, managing time and movement tightly. Don't give the students time to plan what goes wrong each time, but encourage them instead to focus on active listening and responding to their partner each time. The encounters are likely to become more imaginative as the activity goes on.

5 Ask the 'students' (inner circle) how they felt at the end of their 'terrible day', allowing a couple of minutes for whole-class feedback of humorous anecdotes.

6 Now repeat stages 2 to 5 with the inner and outer circles swapping places. This time tell the 'students':

'Yesterday was a brilliant day. Everything went right.'

This may lead to high spirits and positive dynamics.

Variation

This activity is suitable for Business English students to roleplay work context encounters, either on the phone or face to face.

Ordinary People

Level
Lower-intermediate to Advanced

Time
25–35 minutes

Language Links
Personal questions

Aim
To create a chat show and practise questions

1 Sit at the front with the students facing you, sitting in a semi-circle. Tell them that they are the studio audience for a TV chat show. In the manner of a chat show host, address an imaginary camera:

'Hello and welcome to "Ordinary People", the programme where we meet people and ask about their lives and opinions. The special thing about this show is that all the questions come from the audience … And now for our first guest …'

Stand up and lead the applause, then physically become a character different from yourself, acknowledge the applause, sit down and introduce yourself. For example:

'I'm Mrs Joanne Williams, known to my friends as Jo. I've lived on a small farm in the countryside near Cambridge all my life. I'm 87 years old (allow for applause). Now you can ask me whatever you like.'

Encourage questions from the audience which build on information you've already provided to create an in-depth persona. After a few minutes, thank the audience and acknowledge the applause as you stand up and take a seat amongst them.

2 Ask the students to sit in equal-sized semi-circles of between four and seven with an empty chair facing them at the front. Say:

'You are going to be a chat show audience and guests who are ordinary people. Imagine you are a person very different from your real self. Think about your answers to these questions:

● Where are you from? – Be a British person or someone of a different nationality from your own.

● What's your name?

● How old are you?

● What do you do?'

After a minute's thinking time, ask for a volunteer from each group who will open their show as the first guest and sit in the chair facing their group. They should start off by announcing their name, age and where they are from before inviting questions. Remind the audience to listen to the guest's answers and to use them for follow-up questions rather than ask a list of unrelated questions. As each group finishes all their interviews, they can separate and join other groups.

Variation

The interviews can be on a theme being studied, e.g. childhood memories, views on a current topical issue or, in the context of a Business English course, the programme could be called 'People in Business'.

Family Secret

Level

Lower-intermediate to Advanced

Time

30–40 minutes

Language Links

Breaking news

Aim

To create a short family drama

1 Split the class into two equal-sized groups. One group makes a standing inner circle facing outwards, the other makes an outer standing circle facing a partner from the inner circle. If necessary, join in to make an even number. Say:

'You are members of a family, so you are related to the person facing you. Inside is the teenage grandchild, Chris; outside is Chris's gran or grandad. You're in the kitchen talking about the family party tomorrow. You have two minutes to do the scene, OK? 3–2–1 Action.'

2 After two minutes, tell the outer circle students to move one place to the left (clockwise). Say:

'You are members of the same family as before. This time you are Chris, the teenager, on the outside and inside is one of your parents. You're in the living room talking about your gran or grandad's health problem. You have two minutes to do the scene, OK? 3–2–1 Action.'

3 After two minutes, tell the outer circle students to move one place to the left (clockwise). Say:

'You are members of the same family as before. This time you are Chris, the teenager, on the inside, and outside is your younger brother or sister, Sam. You're in Sam's bedroom talking about Sam's problem at school. You have two minutes to do the scene, OK? 3–2–1 Action.'

4 After two minutes, ask the students to sit in groups of four or five, ideally not with people they partnered in stages 1 to 3. They should decide who is Chris, Sam, their mum or dad and gran or grandad (in the case of five people, have Mum *and* Dad). Once they've decided, say:

'In a minute, you're going to do the family party scene. During the party one of you is going to reveal a secret problem to the rest of the family. The secret is not about Gran or Grandad's health problem and it is not about Sam's school problems. It is a problem we don't already know about. This secret will come as a big surprise. It will affect all of you. I'm going to ask you to close your eyes in a moment, and I'm going to touch one person from each group on the shoulder. If I touch you, you are the one with a secret. Don't tell the others if it's you. OK? Close your eyes.'

If possible, select a different family member from each group.

Family Secret

5 Say:

'Now open your eyes. You're in the dining room sitting around the table, eating during the party. You've got five minutes to do the scene. The person with a secret problem is going to tell everybody, but wait a minute before you do. The rest of the scene will be about different people's reactions to the news. Make sure that only one person is talking at a time and that everyone has a chance to speak. At the start of the scene, one of you is arriving late for the party. Make your starting picture, OK? 3–2–1 Action.'

6 After five minutes, say:

'In a moment, you're going to show us the most interesting minute from your scene. Decide which part to show and practise your scene now. Each character will have something to say. Is it the beginning, the middle or the end? OK, bring that one minute to life. Make your starting picture. 3–2–1 Action.'

7 After one minute, quickly reorganise the room so that the audience can sit facing one table. Say:

'Watch and listen to each of the one-minute scenes closely. For each scene I'd like you to try and work out the secret and who else in the family is going to be affected most.'

This gives a listening task to students who might otherwise be focusing on preparing their own scene.

8 After watching all of the short dramas, invite feedback and comments from the whole class.

Parole Board

Level
Intermediate to Advanced

Time
30–45 minutes

Language Links
Expressing regret

Aim
To present an argument, express regret and activate crime vocabulary

1 Form equal-sized groups of between six and ten and sit in a seat facing the whole class. Tell the students they are going to play the roles of prisoners as well as members of a parole board, and make sure they understand the concept. Say:

'The government has ruled that, because of overcrowding, 50 per cent of prisoners have to be released and given the opportunity to make up for their past crimes. You have all been in prison for one year and have been invited before the parole board. If you can explain your crime and why you deserve to go free, you may be lucky.'

2 Elicit and write up more different types of crime than there are students in each group (it's a good idea to exclude sexual assault and abuse) and ask each student in each group to pick a different crime.

3 Choose and announce a crime for yourself which has not been selected by any of the students. Introduce yourself with your criminal identity to the class (the parole board), and, using the prompts in stage 4 below, spend one or two minutes telling your story and trying to justify why you should be released. Make sure you present a borderline case. Give the parole board a minute to ask you further questions before standing up and 'exiting'.

4 Explain that all of the prisoners will be heard before they decide as a group who should get parole. Remind them of their crime and ask them to close their eyes and consider their answers to the following prompt questions. Ask the questions slowly, leaving several seconds between each one:

- What's your name?
- What was your crime?
- Was it your first offence?
- Why did you decide to do this crime?
- How did you prepare for it?
- Did anybody help you?
- What exactly did you do?
- How did you feel when you did it?
- How do you feel about it now?
- How did the police catch you?
- What have you done during your year in prison?
- If you are given parole, what will you do to make up for your past crime or crimes?

5 Ask the students to split into their groups and to arrange the chairs so that one is facing the parole board. Remind them that they each have up to two minutes to tell their story and make their case before facing a minute of questioning. It is not necessary for them to answer all the prompt questions.

6 As each group finishes, give them a time deadline to discuss as parole board members (not criminals) which 50 per cent of the prisoners to release.

Variation
In a Business English class, tell the students they are up for redundancy. Each of them has failed to honour their contract in a different way. They should explain their actions and argue why they are indispensable.

Who's at the Door?

<table>
<tr><td>

Level

Lower-intermediate to Advanced

Time

20–40 minutes

Language Links

Greetings, breaking news

Aim

To respond imaginatively and appropriately in unforeseen situations

</td></tr>
</table>

1 Say:

'You're at home watching TV. The doorbell rings. Who could it be?'

Ask the students to brainstorm possible callers and write up a list of about twenty people, e.g.

- neighbour
- police officer
- child's teacher
- doctor
- beggar
- family member

2 Arrange chairs for half the class (the As) to sit in an inward-facing circle in the middle of the room, imagining they are at home watching TV. Each of the others (the Bs) stands behind a seated partner. Explain that B chooses who to be from the list on board, 'rings the doorbell' and, when A stands up and 'opens the door', initiates a conversation with A as naturally as possible. A has to work out who B is and what he or she wants and respond as naturally as possible. Demonstrate yourself first with a 'quick' student.

3 After 40 seconds, stop them and get the As to guess who the Bs are and what they want. Then ask the Bs to sit down and 'watch TV' and the As to rotate so that they are 'standing at the door' of a new partner. Swap roles and partners for four turns until the game is well established.

4 In the fifth round, develop the game further by telling the students that the Bs have good news for the As and ask them to develop the encounter into a two-minute scene.

5 In the sixth round, after swapping roles, tell the students that the Bs are going to break some bad news and ask them to build another two-minute scene. Freeze them after two minutes and give them one more minute to find a positive resolution.

Optional

(5–15 minutes) Invite willing pairs to perform the final 'bad news and resolution' scene in front of the class.

Role Reversals

Level

Intermediate to Advanced

Time

15–20 minutes

Language Links

Requests and refusals

Aim

To practise negotiating in different status relationships

1 Give each pair of students a chair. Say:

'This is the only chair in the boss's office. It's 8.30 a.m. and the boss's personal secretary, Kim, is waiting for the boss, Chris, to arrive. Kim and Chris are on first-name terms although there is a big difference in status. Chris is coming in the door. Freeze in position. Each of you might be holding something. What could it be? When I say "Action", begin the scene and talk about Chris's journey to work. When I say "Freeze", freeze in position, OK? 3–2–1 Action.'

2 After a minute, freeze all the pairs and ask Chris and Kim to look at how the other is standing and change places, exactly copying their partner's posture and expression. Say:

'When I say "Action", continue from where I froze you. If you were Kim before, now you are Chris and the other way round. Talk about your work plans for today. 3–2–1 Action.'

3 After each of the following turns below, freeze the pairs and ask them to swap roles:

- Kim politely asks Chris for some time off. Chris wants to know all the details before deciding.

- Chris says no politely and explains why. Kim politely tries to change Chris's mind.

- (The end of the same day) Kim comes into Chris's office to say goodbye. They don't talk about Kim's request.

- Final scene. Chris or Kim starts talking about the request again. There is a happy or unhappy ending and Kim leaves.

4 Ask the students to replay the whole story, freezing and swapping roles at the same points (this time without you telling them to). Now, the student who began the scene as Kim begins as Chris and vice versa. They should try to stick closely to the story but the dialogue will obviously change.

Optional

(5–10 minutes) Ask the students to show parts of their scenes to the whole class, i.e. pair one shows section one, pair two section two, etc. Try to make sure you see different endings, ideally at least one happy and one unhappy.

Variation

Use any similar scenario where there is an obvious difference in status, e.g. teacher and student, parent and teenager.

Did You Hear?

Level

Lower-intermediate to Advanced

Time

15–20 minutes

Language Links

Giving news, expressing surprise

Aim

To practise passing on and exaggerating rumours

1 Elicit the types of rumour that spread quickly through social circles, e.g. a couple breaking up, someone losing their job, someone winning some money, etc. Drill the question opener 'Did you hear that John ...?' and invite a confident student to give you a made-up piece of gossip. Respond by asking for more details, then go on to another student and pass on the rumour, slightly exaggerating the details.

2 Put the students in pairs, A and B, and ask the As to start off a made-up rumour about one or more made-up characters. Tell the Bs to listen and ask for details before finding another A and passing on the rumour in a slightly exaggerated way. A continues by spreading the rumour to another B.

3 After five minutes, ask all the Bs to take the last rumour they heard and try to find the A-student who started it. It may be hard to recognise!

4 Finally put the students in small groups and invite them to exchange real-life experiences of rumours and their feelings about them.

Receiving Presents

Level

Lower-intermediate to Advanced

Time

15–20 minutes

Language Links

Thanking

Aim

To practise giving and receiving presents and apologies

1 Ask the students to stand in a circle. Approach a confident student and improvise (with mime) receiving a present from them. Say: 'Is that for me? Thank you. Oh, it's so nicely wrapped. It's quite an unusual shape, isn't it? Can I open it now?' etc. Be genuinely surprised and pleased or pretend to be. Ask how/where they found it and tell them what you'll do with it. In this activity, it's the receiver who decides and makes it clear what the present is.

2 Ask the students to stand in A and B pairs. Say:

'In the next three minutes, the Bs are going to receive a present from the As. Whether you really like it or not, you will show that you are delighted and say what you'll do with it.'

3 After three minutes, tell the Bs that it's a couple of days later and the friend who gave them the present has come to visit them at home. They are going to ask about the present, but unfortunately there's a small problem.

4 After two or three minutes, repeat stages 2 and 3 with the As receiving presents from a different B-partner.

5 Ask the whole class: 'Whose problem was not really small?' 'Are you still friends?' etc. This is a good opportunity to discuss the rituals surrounding the giving of presents.

Strong Feelings

Level
Lower-intermediate to Advanced

Time
10–15 minutes

Language Links
Expressing strong emotions

Aim
To practise expressing strong feelings

1 Introduce the activity by telling the students that they are going to communicate some strong feelings in a series of one-minute scenes. Tell them to find a partner. Say:

'First, you are going to tell your child that their lovely dog, Lucky, is dead. 3–2–1 Action.' (*Grief*)

It is not necessary to allocate roles as they are established the moment one of the pair initiates the exchange.

2 Ask the students to do as many of the scenes below as seem appropriate. After each one-minute scene, stop all the pairs and ask them to find a new partner. The briefing should be short and clear. Don't mention the emotions given in brackets. Finish on a high with the last one or two.

- You get home and the babysitter has left your baby at home alone. Now the babysitter comes in. (*Anger*)

- You've given away the new watch which your friend gave you. Your friend asks about the watch. (*Guilt*)

- You arrive home with your flatmate. You can hear somebody moving around noisily in the bedroom. (*Fear*)

- It's late in the evening and you're a young person who's lost your wallet or purse. At the bus stop, ask to borrow £2 for your bus fare from a middle-aged person, who doesn't believe your story. (*Mistrust*)

- You tell a kind stranger on a bus about a personal problem. (*Sympathy*)

- You are two elderly people in the post office. You recognise each other. You were best friends at school. (*Delight*)

- Your boss is very pleased and is going to give you a pay rise. (*Satisfaction*)

3 Elicit the types of strong feelings (as indicated above) which have been acted out. Invite comments on how it felt to express strong emotions in English.

Telephone Hotseat

Level
Lower-intermediate to Advanced

Time
15 minutes

Language Links
Telephoning

Aim
To manage two conversations at the same time

1 Put the students in groups of three and allocate these roles: Pat, Pat's mother or father, Pat's boyfriend or girlfriend. Seat the students so that Pat is facing his or her boy/girlfriend and the parent is facing Pat's back.

2 Say:

'Pat, your mother or father wants to talk to you on the phone about their problems but, just after you start speaking, your boy/girlfriend has an immediate problem that cannot wait. You are going to have two conversations at the same time. You've got three minutes. Hold your phones (gesture). Ready? The phone's ringing NOW.'

3 After three minutes, ask the groups to discuss the skills and problems involved in keeping two conversations going at the same time.

4 Discuss with the whole class any real-life experiences of this situation.

Optional

(5 minutes) Have two further rounds so that everyone has a turn at managing two conversations. Use these situations:

1 Jackie's boss is phoning Jackie at home about a work problem and Jackie's neighbour comes round with an immediate problem.

2 Georgie is at the office. His/her child is on the phone with a personal problem and Georgie's secretary has an immediate problem.

Variation

In a business context, there are numerous different colleagues, clients and suppliers who might call or meet you in the office, over lunch, on the train, etc. At the office you could build up to dealing with two or more callers and a face-to-face meeting (and why not throw in video conferencing?) for a real test of multi-conversation skills.

Homeless Traveller

Level
   Lower-intermediate to Advanced

Time
   15–25 minutes

Language Links
   Asking questions and showing compassion

Aim
   To practise talking about personal problems and showing understanding

1 Put the students in pairs, A and B, and ask them to put their chairs close together next to each other like park benches. Ask all the Bs to stand up. Say to them:

'B, you're travelling around the USA and now you're in San Francisco, walking by the docks. You see a man sitting on a bench, looking at the sea and watching the ships. He looks very lonely, like a homeless traveller. You decide to sit on the bench next to him and ask him about his lifestory, his problems and his plans. Don't give him any advice, just listen to his story and try to understand. A, you're the man on the bench. You've got five minutes, OK? 3–2–1 Action.'

2 At the end of the five minutes, say:

'In a moment you're going to show us the most interesting minute from your scene, OK? Make the starting picture for your minute and do that minute again to prepare. 3–2–1 Action.'

3 When they are ready, pairs show their one-minute extracts to the rest of the class.

NOTE: I devised this activity as a lead-in for the song 'Sittin' on the Dock of the Bay' by Otis Redding.

Jilted Lover

Level
Lower-intermediate to Advanced

Level

Lower-intermediate to Advanced

Time

15–25 minutes

Language Links

Accusing and denying

Aim

To practise accusing and denying and discussing relationships

NOTE: The make-up of the class and the relationships among the students will determine whether or not you do this activity and how you might form the pairs.

1 Put the students in pairs and say:

'You are in love with a beautiful person. You have been together for several months and it's been wonderful. You have been incredibly happy. But yesterday a friend of yours told you that they had heard that the person you love is seeing someone else, someone that they went out with before you met. You don't want to believe what your friend says, but in your heart you think it might be true. You are at home and you know that any minute your love is coming home. You really don't want to lose them so you don't want to get angry, but you need to know the truth. Even if they say it's not true, you don't know if you can believe them. Stand with your partner and decide who is who and what your names are. OK, you've got five minutes to do the scene. 3–2–1 Action.'

2 At the end of the five minutes, say:

'In a moment you're going to show us the most interesting minute from your scene. Make the starting picture for your minute and do that minute again to prepare. 3–2–1 Action.'

3 When they are ready, invite pairs to show their one-minute extracts in turn.

NOTE: I devised this activity as a lead-in to the song 'I Heard It Through the Grapevine' by Marvin Gaye.

40

Designer Home

Level

Intermediate to Advanced

Time

20–25 minutes

Language Links

Asking for and giving advice

Aim

To practise asking for and making suggestions about house design

1 Ask all the students to stand in groups of three and tell them that they are Sid and Sarah Smith and Jude Jones. Say:

'Sid and Sarah Smith, your neighbour Jude Jones's house is exactly the same as yours, but he or she has spent the last few months redesigning, renovating, redecorating and refurnishing it. Jude has invited you round to show you the house now it's finished. Jude is extremely proud and thinks you should do similar things to your house. Sid, you really don't like what Jude has done because you like the traditional character of your house. Also you're lazy when it comes to DIY. Sarah, you love some of the things Jude has done and would like Sid to help you to make the same changes to your own house, but there are some other things you hate. Of course neither of you wants to hurt Jude's feelings so you can only say what you really think when Jude's leading the way into the next room. You've got eight minutes, OK? 3–2–1 Action.'

2 At the end of the eight minutes, say:

'In a moment you're going to show us the most interesting minute from your scene, OK? Make the starting picture for your minute and do that minute again to prepare. 3–2–1 Action.'

3 When they are ready, the groups take turns to show their one-minute extracts to the rest of the class.

Variation

To activate clothes vocabulary, Jude could show off a complete new wardrobe of designer clothes to friends and suggest that they should update their wardrobes in a similar way.

Roof Sketches

Level

    Lower-intermediate to Advanced

Time

    20–25 minutes

Language Links

    Persuading and giving orders

Aim

    To improvise and perform a sketch

1 Describe (or, if possible, indicate out of the window) a large house. Tell the students that you saw three strangers on the roof the day before and ask them to speculate about who they were and what they might have been doing. Encourage imaginative answers, e.g. neighbours rescuing a pet cat, burglars, etc. Write each situation on the board.

2 Put the students in groups of three (you can join a group to make up the numbers if necessary). Each member of a group chooses one of these three character types: 1 Leader, 2 Nervous, 3 Practical and each group chooses a situation from the board.

3 Ask each group to make a frozen tableau of the three characters balancing on the edge of the roof and then improvise their sketch. After a couple of minutes, give them 30 seconds to come to an exciting ending.

4 Tell the students they are going to perform to the rest of the class in a couple of minutes and ask them to replay their sketches in preparation, starting and finishing with a frozen tableau.

5 Encourage each group in turn to perform their sketch. Make sure the other groups listen carefully and ask them afterwards to identify the situation and say which of the three roles each of the students was playing.

Family Crisis

Level

Lower-intermediate to Advanced

Time

20–35 minutes

Language Links

Breaking delicate news

Aim

To create a family crisis sketch

1 Put the students in groups of three and allocate the following roles:

A: Mr or Mrs Pink – British parent of Sally, a female university student

B: Sally Pink – British student at London University, bringing her new boyfriend home in the middle of the term

C: Roger Smith – Sally's new boyfriend

If any students are left over, they can play Jackie Pink, Sally's younger brother or sister who still lives at home.

2 Ask B and C to discuss their relationship briefly while the As get together from different groups to discuss how British parents might react to their daughter's new boyfriend.

3 Start the improvised roleplay with B and C ringing A's doorbell. Allow the improvisation to progress for a few minutes before suggesting that A and B may want to talk in private as B has some VERY IMPORTANT NEWS (in my experience, most students opt either for pregnancy or for dropping out of university to live with their boyfriend). Remove the Cs and tell them that they are now the other parent of another group's B, then let them 'arrive home' to have the news broken by their wife/husband and daughter.

4 Finally, stop the groups and allow one group at a time to show or improvise what happens when Roger re-enters the scene, making a group of four. This means that the person originally playing Roger returns to their first group and encounters their girlfriend's other parent for the first time. Each C student will, therefore, appear in two different scenes, once as Roger and once as the second parent. By now the students will be fully engaged in the improvisation and unlikely to be embarrassed at performing in front of the others without rehearsal.

Love Triangle

Level
Intermediate to Advanced

Time
30–35 minutes

Language Links
Describing relationships

Aim
To create a short relationship drama .

1 Draw a large triangle on the board and write the names Jack, Sue and Pete at the corners. Elicit the idea of a love triangle. Establish that Jack and Sue are married but that Sue isn't happy; that Jack and Pete are best friends and that Sue and Pete are secret lovers, but Pete wants Sue to tell Jack and leave him. Ask for (and write up around the triangle) details like ages, jobs, how Jack and Pete know each other and what they do together socially, and when and where Pete and Sue meet in secret.

2 Ask all the students to stand up in pairs and to decide who is Jack and who is Sue (depending on the make-up and cultural backgrounds of the class you might or might not ask for male/female pairs). Say:

'It's 10 p.m. Jack's getting home late at the end of a busy day. Sue is upset but wants to keep her affair with Pete secret. OK? 3–2–1 Action.'

After two minutes, stop the students and invite quick feedback.

3 Ask the students to make new pairs with a different partner; they are now Jack and Pete. Tell them they are together socially (according to earlier input, e.g. playing golf). Jack wants to talk about his marriage problems and Pete has

promised Sue to keep their affair secret.

After they have brought the scene to life for two minutes, stop them and invite feedback.

4 Ask the students to find a new partner and to be Sue and Pete. Say:

'Sue and Pete are meeting where they always meet. Sue is arriving late. Pete tries to persuade Sue to tell Jack but Sue refuses. OK? 3–2–1 Action.'

After two minutes stop them and invite feedback.

5 Ask the students to make new groups of three. Establish that it is late in the evening. Sue and Jack are in the living room. There is an unexpected knock at the front door. Pete has decided to tell Jack about his affair with Sue and to ask Sue to leave with him. Of course, Sue will try to stop Pete from telling Jack. A couple of minutes into the scene (or longer if all the groups are still going strong), stop the students and give them one more minute to find a conclusion to the drama.

6 Ask all the groups to replay the last scene simultaneously in just two minutes, making sure it will be clear for the others to understand, before asking them to show each other their dramatic scenes and their various outcomes.

Variation

In a Business English class, J and P could be the owners of long-term rival clothing manufacturing companies who are on friendly terms and often socialise together. S owns a chain of fashion stores and has always been loyal to J as his or her main supplier, but is now in secret negotiations with P, who is offering a better deal. In the final scene, P arrives unexpectedly at S's office during a regular meeting between S and J. P announces the deal even though S hasn't yet committed to it or signed any contract.

Dicey Sketches

Level

Lower-Intermediate to Advanced

Time

40–45 minutes

Materials

Dice (one for every three or four students)

Language Links

Dealing with problems

Aim

To improvise a sketch about a problem

1 Brainstorm and write on the board one list of characters and one of places, each numbered 1–6. For example:

1 Tourist	1 Street corner
2 Police officer	2 In a bank
3 Drunk	3 Riverside
4 Shopper	4 Pub
5 Business person	5 On the bus
6 Beggar	6 Supermarket

2 Put the students in groups of three or four and give each group a dice. Each student rolls the dice to find out their identity and the dice is rolled once again to decide on a location (e.g. a shopper and two beggars in a pub). Groups quickly decide if any of the characters know each other and, if so, what their relationship is.

3 Tell two members of each group that they have been together in the location for a couple of minutes and to freeze in role, then to bring the scene to life. At an appropriate moment (after a minute or two) the other group member joins them and continues the roleplay.

4 After a couple of minutes, stop all the groups. Tell them that a problem is going to arise in the scene. (If a problem has already come up, they will have to deal with a second one!) Write up a numbered list of problems. For example:

1 death
2 mistake
3 fall
4 fight
5 money
6 broken heart

Each group's dice is then rolled and the group must incorporate the allotted problem as they improvise the next part of the roleplay.

5 At an appropriate moment, stop the groups and tell them they have one minute to find an unexpected ending to their roleplay.

6 Now that they have improvised a whole sketch, the groups have a few minutes to replay and adapt their sketches before performing them for the other groups.

Memories

Level

Lower-intermediate to Advanced

Time

15–20 minutes

Materials

Nostalgic music (e.g. Enya)

Language Links

Discussing memories

Aim

To create an improvised dialogue about memories

1 Get the students to sit comfortably in pairs and to close their eyes. Play a short extract from a piece of music which might evoke a sense of nostalgia. Ask the students how it makes them feel.

2 Tell the pairs they are adult siblings at home and that they're doing a piece of housework together, e.g. washing and drying up, ironing and folding clothes, etc. Get them to mime their actions fairly slowly with the music playing.

3 Stop the music. Tell them that, while working, they're going to share a sad memory from many years ago and talk about their feelings then and now. Play the piece again and make sure each pair continues miming while they talk.

4 Without stopping the music, tell them that the sad memory leads them on to the memory of a much happier event. Let them recall this together.

5 Finally get each pair to recall their sad and happy memories with music and actions while the others watch and listen.

Variation

If you feel this may be too sensitive, in stage 3 ask one of the pair to talk about an imaginary personal problem and the other to ask for details. In stage 4 their partner suggests a solution which is gladly received.

Car Break-in

Level
Lower-intermediate to Advanced

Time
25–30 minutes

Language Links
Reported speech and reporting verbs

Aim
To improvise and report back on a suspicious event

1 Ask the students to stand in pairs, A and B. Say:

'A, you are an eighteen-year-old British student living in London. Your uncle is an internationally famous actor (decide which one). He has lent you his priceless 1960s Rolls Royce while he's in Hollywood for a couple of weeks. It's 9 p.m. and you've just parked the car near Trafalgar Square, but you've locked yourself out. The keys and your bag with all your money and documents in it are inside the car. You've left the window a little bit open, so you're going to try to get back in. When you see a police officer, ask him or her to help you.

B, you're a police officer. You see a young person trying to break into a priceless beautiful old Rolls Royce. They tell you a story, but it's very difficult to believe. You've got five minutes to act out the scene. Listen carefully to your partner and try to remember everything they say. OK? 3–2–1 Action.'

After four minutes tell the pairs they have one minute to find an interesting ending to their scene.

2 Tell the students that in a moment they're going to show the last minute of their scene to the rest of the class. Remind them that they know what they're going to say, so they should practise again, focusing on body language and feelings. After a minute, ask the students to watch each other's scenes carefully and note the differences in the outcomes. Divide a large class into sixes or eights for this.

3 Ask the A-students to sit with a different B-student. Say:

'B, you're the same police officer. It's a week later and one of your police colleagues, A, has just got back from holiday. You're in the police station canteen. A asks you if anything interesting happened while they were away. Tell them the Rolls Royce story and report the conversation from your point of view. A, how are you going to react to this story? OK? 3–2–1 Action.'

4 Ask the A-students to stand with yet another B-student. Say:

'A, you're the student. It's two weeks later. You go to Heathrow Airport to meet your uncle, the internationally famous actor, in Arrivals. He asks about his Rolls Royce. Tell him the story and report the conversation with the police officer from your point of view. B, you're the uncle. How are you going to react? OK? 3–2–1 Action.'

5 Invite comments and examples from the whole class about how the details of a story change over time. Do they have any real-life examples of this?

Death at the Manor

<table>
<tr><td>

Level

Intermediate to Advanced

Time

60–70 minutes

Language Links

Further-information questions

Aim

To create a murder mystery drama

</td></tr>
</table>

NOTE: The class should comprise between six and 12 students. If students are unfamiliar with British whodunits, it may be a good idea to look at or read an example together before doing this activity.

1 Draw a big house on the board and explain that it is an old British country manor house. Tell the students it is 3 p.m. on a Friday last summer and that they are approaching the house. Elicit a detailed description of:

- the outside and gardens
- the entrance hall
- the main sitting room

Then tell the students that this is the home of the Scott-Parker family. Ask them who lives there and who works there. Elicit and write up at least seven characters' names, ages and lengths of connection to the family.

2 Ask the students to visualise a dead body behind the sofa in the sitting room. They decide which one of the characters is the victim, which one has discovered the body and phoned the police, and how the victim was murdered.

3 Agree which of the characters are suspects (these must be half the number of students in the class) and tell the students to ignore the others. Ask the students to work in pairs. Each pair chooses a different suspect and decides on his or her possible motives for the murder. Get feedback from the whole class after a few minutes.

4 Ask the students to divide into two equal-sized groups: suspects and detectives. The class must agree and be clear about who is playing which suspect. Tell them that all the suspects were at the manor but were not together with anyone else when the murder was committed.

5 All the students close their eyes while you silently and secretly select the murderer with a touch on the shoulder.

6 Tell them that all the suspects should act a bit suspiciously, but that the innocent ones need to be consistent in their stories. The murderer can be as devious as he or she likes. Ask the students to work in detective/suspect pairs and give them a minute of silent preparation for the pairwork interrogations. Tell the detectives that they should focus on motives rather than means.

Death at the Manor

7 Tell the students it is now 4 p.m. and the detective/suspect pairs must now roleplay interviews.

8 Ask the detectives to confer and decide which suspect to take in for further questioning. Meanwhile the suspects meet, speculate about each other's guilt and accuse each other.

9 Tell the detectives that they may ask a few more questions in open class before agreeing on their chief suspect.

10 The chief suspect is then arrested and interrogated by the detectives. If they have the wrong person, the teacher may supply some evidence to prove their innocence, e.g. their shoes are muddy but no footprints were found near the body.

11 Finally the murderer's identity is revealed and he or she explains why and how the murder was committed.

True Friendship?

Level
> Lower-intermediate to Advanced

Time
> 15–25 minutes

Language Links
> Informal expressions

Aim
> To improvise a conversation between friends involving a moral dilemma

1 Put the students into pairs, A and B. Say:

'You're walking home with a friend and you're both hungry. A stops to buy two chocolate bars and gives one to B. B unwraps the chocolate bar and inside finds a prize-winning voucher for £1,000. B really needs the money – think why. A is looking the other way so he or she doesn't know about the voucher and thinks B just has a normal chocolate bar. B, think how you feel. OK, make a frozen picture of the moment. B, you're looking at the voucher you've just found. You're probably going to put it in your pocket. A, think about what you're looking at. Remember you've both got a chocolate bar. FREEZE. In a moment you're going to bring the scene to life. This scene will tell us about A and B's friendship and their lives. You have three minutes, OK? 3–2–1 Action.'

Give them a 30 seconds-to-go warning and at the end count down to a frozen picture.

2 It's a good idea for students to replay a scene before showing it. Say:

'Now do the same scene again. This time, you know what happens, so focus on the words and your body language. Make your starting picture. 3–2–1 Action.'

3 Ask different pairs to talk about the outcome of their scene and the nature of the friendship. Give pairs with different outcomes the chance to show a one-minute extract from their scene in front of the class. Invite comments about B's body language in the scenes where B is not completely honest, and those where B tells A about the voucher.

Optional

Have a follow-up discussion about what class members would actually do in these circumstances.

Mediation

Level

    Lower-intermediate to Advanced

Time

    10 minutes

Language Links

    Complaining and negotiating

Aim

    To practise complaints and negotiating
    between neighbours

Variations

In a Business English class, the three can be colleagues of similar status. Alternatively, teenagers could play disputing parents and a teenage son or daughter, although this may be a very sensitive subject.

1 Ask the students to form groups of three; they are neighbours, Alex, Billy and Chris. Sit Alex and Billy on opposite sides of the room. Say:

'Alex and Billy used to be friendly neighbours but they have had a row and stopped talking to each other. They have a lot of complaints about each other's lifestyle. Chris is a neighbour and friend of both and has five minutes to go between the two and resolve the quarrel. 3–2–1 Action.'

2 After five minutes, ask Chris to bring Alex and Billy together and allow another couple of minutes for them to make up (or not, as the case may be).

3 Find out if any students have experience of mediation.

Gossips

Level

Lower-intermediate to Advanced

Time

15 minutes

Language Links

Reacting to news

Aim

To explore the possible consequences of gossip

1 Ask the students to sit in pairs. Check that they all understand 'gossip', and find out if they enjoy gossiping about people they know (they might deny it). Say:

'Imagine you both do the same thing, for example you're both maths teachers or you're both Manchester United football players or you're both students in the same art class. OK? Quickly decide who you are, your names and where you are.'

After a few seconds say:

'It's Friday afternoon and you both love gossiping. You're going to gossip about one person you both know. OK? Begin.'

2 After three or four minutes, stop the pairs and invite whole-class feedback. Find out the juiciest bit of gossip from each pair.

3 Say:

'The person who you were gossiping about overheard the whole conversation and is upset because some of the things you said are not true. A little while later, he or she has decided to come to talk to one of you about this.'

One of the pair becomes the 'gossip victim' and starts the two-minute conversation.

4 After two minutes, invite some pairs to show the whole class an extract from this last exchange.

5 As a whole class, discuss the possible consequences of gossip and, if it seems appropriate, the students' own experiences.

Excuses

Level

Lower-intermediate to Advanced

Time

10 minutes

Language Links

Making excuses

Aim

To practise making and elaborating
on excuses

Variation

In a Business English class, employees can make
excuses to their boss.

1 Ask the students to stand in equal-sized groups of
between four and seven, and place the
appropriate number of chairs for each group in
two rows, all facing the same way. Say:

'One of you is a teacher. The English class has
started and most of the students are there, but the
rest of you are all late. You're going to come in
one at a time and sit down as quietly as possible,
but the teacher will ask each of you why you are
late. Each one of you must give a different,
realistic excuse and answer the teacher's
questions about it. Be as polite as you can.'

2 Ask each of the teachers to stand facing their
group of chairs, establish where the imaginary
door to each classroom is and ask the other group
members to stand behind it before starting the
scene. As each group finishes, ask them to
evaluate which the most successful excuses were
and who was most polite to the teacher.

The Lift

1 Arrange the chairs so that they make enclosed spaces (lifts) of about 1 metre square. There should be one lift for every group of three or four students. Divide the students into groups and assign roles: A is Anna or Andy, B is Beth or Bill, C is Claire or Colin, D is Diane or Donald. Give each group a minute to decide if they are friends, family or colleagues, what building the lift is in, whether they're going up or down, and where they're going.

2 After a minute, say: 'OK, the lift is coming. Let the other people out before you get in. And remember to stand facing the door. 3–2–1 Action.' When everyone is in and all the lifts are moving, indicate with a noise and a large gesture that the lift has got stuck between floors. Allow the scene to develop for three or four minutes, before indicating that the lift has started moving again.

3 Say:

'I'd like you to do part of the scene again, from the moment the lift gets stuck to when it starts again. But this time it's only going to be two minutes. Afterwards you're going to show it to the other groups, so please speak clearly and only one person can speak at a time, OK? Get ready. 3–2–1 Action.'

4 After two minutes, each group performs the lift breakdown scene in turn. Ask the others to try to work out the relationship between the characters and to decide where they're going.

Airport Goodbyes

Level
> Lower-intermediate to Advanced

Time
> 10–20 minutes

Language Links
> Goodbyes

Aim
> To practise personal goodbyes and explore body language

1 Ask the students to stand in pairs, A and B. Say:

'You are close friends saying goodbye in front of passport control at the airport. What are your names? A is leaving and you won't see each other for a very long time. Think what you want to say to your friend before you go. A, you have two minutes before you have to go through passport control. OK? 3–2–1 Action.'

Give the students a 20-second warning before the end, so A can physically walk away.

2 After very brief feedback and comments on the students' real-life experiences of this situation, say:

'Now, you're going to have exactly the same conversation again with exactly the same words. The only difference is that this time you both really want to say goodbye to your friend because you've had enough of each other. You really need a break from each other. In fact, in your heart, you don't mind if you never see your friend again. But of course, you don't really want your friend to know this, so you will say all the same things. There may be a difference in your voice,

your intonation, your body language and especially how much eye-contact you give. Do you think you'll need more or less time than before? This time you'll only need 90 seconds. OK? 3–2–1 Action.'

At the end, invite comments on differences and feelings from the whole class.

3 (Optional) Ask the students to do a third version of the scene in which they each have different feelings about saying goodbye. Before starting, they decide which of them wants to say goodbye and which of them doesn't. Once they've done the scene, invite a few pairs to perform their scene and ask the others to listen and watch and note body language.

Bringing Photos to Life

Level

Elementary to Advanced

Time

15–20 minutes

Materials

At least one photo per pair of students, each showing a different pair of people conversing

Language Links

General conversation

Aim

To improvise a conversation and listen actively

1 Ask the students to stand in pairs, away from the other pairs. Hold the photos out face down while a member of each pair comes up and takes one, making sure no one else sees it. Each pair looks at their photo and decides who is going to be who. Give them five seconds to make a frozen tableau of the photo. Remove the photos.

2 Tell the pairs to 'bring their photo to life', making sure they don't talk *about* the photo but roleplay the *people in* the photo. They can move around if they wish. After two minutes, ask them to freeze in position.

3 Ask the students to repeat the process in one minute, this time editing and improving the dialogue ready to show other pairs. Make sure they start with the frozen image.

4 Get each pair to re-enact their 60-second scene in turn. Tell the other pairs to watch and listen carefully and 'imagine' the photo so that afterwards they can identify it.

5 After all the pairs have finished, spread out all the photos (including any unused ones) on a table. Ask the students to spend a minute individually deciding (*without* speaking or pointing) which photos the other pairs represented. Finally, the students talk together and agree which photos were brought to life and by whom.

Voicing Thoughts

Level

Lower-intermediate to Advanced

Time

20–35 minutes

Materials

A suitable photo which shows at least five people distinctly

Language Links

Expressing feelings

Aim

To voice other people's secret thoughts

1 Show the whole class a photo of at least five people, e.g. a family watching TV. Put the students into equal-sized groups of four or five and ask them to recreate the image, each member of the group representing a different person in the photo.

2 Tell the students that they are going to voice their person's thoughts at that moment for one minute. Point out that people often think about things unrelated to the moment, and that they might think about two or three different things at almost the same time. All the students should speak simultaneously for one minute.

3 Ask one group to make the frozen photo image again, while the others sit and observe. Another group's members in turn speak the thoughts of the different characters, while the focus of the class remains on the frozen image. After the characters have 'spoken', the observers guess which thoughts were whose.

4 Repeat stage 3 for each of the groups.

Mini Dramas

Level

Lower-intermediate to Advanced

Time

20–25 minutes

Materials

Photos showing at least two characters from a movie or TV drama (movie/TV magazines often have these). You will need enough for each member of the class to play a character. Avoid very well-known dramas.

Language Links

Expressing strong feelings

Aim

To create a short dramatic scene

1 Put the students in groups of two to five, depending on the photos you have brought, and ask them to sit apart from other groups. Give each group a photo from a movie or TV drama showing the same number of people as there are students in the group. Each group looks at the photo (without letting the other groups see it) and decides who is going to be who. Give the groups five seconds to recreate the frozen images.

2 Tell the groups that something unexpected and dramatic is about to happen in their scene. Ask them to bring their frozen images to life simultaneously with dialogue. After two minutes get them to freeze.

3 Ask the students to repeat the process in *one* minute, improving the dialogue ready to show the other groups. Make sure they start with the original frozen tableaux.

4 Now ask the groups to imagine the scene one minute *before* the original picture and make new tableaux. Ask them to decide whether they would all be present. Tell them to bring these scenes to life and to finish with the original image in one minute. As they come to the end, count down 5–4–3–2–1.

5 Now get the students to put the whole two-minute sequence together without stopping in the middle but starting and finishing with their own frozen tableaux.

6 Ask each group to perform their scene while the others watch and listen.

7 Spread out the photos and get the groups to identify the other groups' photos and to comment on their performances.

The Magic Book

Level

Lower-intermediate to Advanced

Time

25–35 minutes

Materials

One plain-covered, blank book for every four or five students and 'magical music' (e.g. Enya or the soundtrack to the film *Chocolat*).

Language Links

Past narrative tenses

Aim

To listen to other students and, as a class, create and tell a tale of magic

1 Form a seated circle and put on extended 'magical' background music (I use Enya's *Watermark*). Tell the students you are going to tell them a magic story from the Magic Book.

Open one of the books (so they can't see the blank pages) and 'read' aloud in a gentle, mysterious voice. I sometimes begin: 'Once a very, very long time ago in a land far, far away a young man, Simon, started a long journey …'

Then ask the students a question, such as 'Why?' Accept the first answer (unless it is silly) and continue 'reading' the story, incorporating the students' input while now and again asking for further input with such questions as 'Who did he meet next?' 'What did she tell him?' or 'Describe the house.' Always accept every contribution as long as it doesn't sabotage the storyline, and make sure there is a problem that requires a solution at the heart of the story. Don't forget to turn the pages as you 'read'. This first stage can go on for at least four or five minutes.

2 Once you have established that the Magic Book creates the story on the page as you read, you can solemnly hold out the book and a volunteer student can take it and continue. Make sure they also solicit and incorporate all the other students' ideas. It may be a good idea for you or the storyteller sometimes to recap recent developments in the story for clarification.

3 Once a few students have 'read', prompt the next storyteller to reincorporate events and characters from earlier in the story and resolve the problem. When the story is finished, you can produce more Magic Books (one per group of four or five students) and each group can read its own magic tale.

Variation

With some classes, you might decide to keep the role of storyteller throughout. Even if you do, students will still feel really involved, especially if you encourage contributions from them all.

The Glove

Level

Lower-intermediate to Advanced

Time

25–30 minutes

Materials

A large black glove or hat for every four or five students and 'spooky music' (e.g. Peter Gabriel's *Passion*).

Language Links

Past narrative tenses

Aim

To listen to other students and, as a class, create and tell a spooky tale

NOTE: If you have already tried *The Magic Book*, here is another way of using a simple prop and music as stimuli, this time to make a spooky tale.

1 Form a seated circle and put on extended 'spooky' background music (I use Peter Gabriel's *Passion*). Tell the students you are going to tell them a story and place the glove (or hat) on the floor in front of you. Speaking in the first person, I usually begin in a spooky voice:

'One dark cold evening a couple of winters ago, I was driving home though a forest, when I suddenly saw something large right in front of the car. I stopped as quickly as I could, got out and went to see, but the only thing I found on the road was (picking the glove or hat up slowly) … It was completely quiet. I was freezing cold so (put the glove/hat on) … At that moment I thought I heard something move in the trees near the road so I went to look …'

Ask the students a question, such as 'What did I find?' Accept the first answer (unless it is silly) and continue the story, incorporating the student input while now and again asking for further input with such questions as 'What did I do next?' 'What did the voice say?' or 'Describe the old woman.' Accept every contribution. The storyline can go in any direction, but remember that a good story generally includes a central problem that needs resolving.

2 Once you have established that the glove (or hat) is integral to the whole story, hold it out solemnly and a volunteer student can take it and continue. The glove (or hat) can be held or worn by the storyteller. Make sure he or she solicits and incorporates the other students' ideas. At the end of the turn, recap, or invite another student to recap, the main developments in the story.

3 Once a few students have taken on the role of storyteller, guide the story towards an ending by prompting the next storyteller to reincorporate events and characters from earlier in the story and to deal with the main problem. When the story has ended, produce more gloves and/or hats (one per group of four or five students) and each group can tell its own spooky tale.

Story Perspectives

Level
Intermediate to Advanced

Time
30–35 minutes

Language Links
Past narrative tenses

Aim
To retell and dramatise a well-known story

Preparation

Before the lesson, practise telling the story of Little Red Riding Hood. Prepare to tell the story in two halves. Tell the first half from the point of view of the wolf up until he has eaten Grandma. Tell the second half from Little Red Riding Hood's point of view, including when she joins her grandma in the wolf's stomach. Find your own unique way of telling the story (if you need a reminder, there are plenty of versions on the internet). As you practise, focus on the distinct postures, movements, voices and styles of speech you will use for each character. Use direct speech and vivid descriptions to bring the story alive. With a little preparation, we teachers are capable of being wonderful storytellers.

1 Stand at the front and ask the students to enjoy listening to a familiar story told in a new way. Once you have finished, elicit the fact that you didn't tell the story as a third person narrator, but from the two different main characters' perspectives.

2 Put the students in pairs and ask them to decide which character each one will play. Say:

'Little Red Riding Hood is going to tell Part One up until she arrives at Grandma's cottage. The wolf will tell Part Two. While you are telling your part of the story, your partner can help and support as long as they do it in character.'

3 When they have all finished the story, ask half the pairs to act out the scene of Little Red Riding Hood and the wolf meeting in the forest and the other pairs to act out the scene of Little Red Riding Hood and the wolf in Grandma's cottage (the wolf can recline on one or two chairs for this). Say 'After your three-minute practice, you're going to show another pair. OK? Begin.'

4 After three minutes, put each forest-scene pair with a cottage-scene pair to show each other their scenes. When they have finished, ask each group of four to act out the end of the story as the woodcutter, the wolf, Little Red Riding Hood and Grandma.

Variation

This activity can be adapted to almost any story with at least two main characters.

Questions Story

Level

Lower-intermediate to Advanced

Time

25–30 minutes

Language Links

Closed questions

Aim

To create and dramatise a story and demonstrate to students that they do have imagination

1 Form a seated circle. Tell the students (deceitfully) that you have a story in your head that they must guess by asking yes/no questions. Just tell them that there are two main characters called Tom and Jessica. Initially, guide the types of question by saying 'First find out about the relationship between Tom and Jessica, who they are, where they are and when the story is set.' It will be natural for students to use present tenses at this stage. At first give more 'Yes' answers to build the students' confidence. Answer 'No' to questions that conflict with the development of the story (this is all quite subjective), but avoid steering the story. Invite questions from all the class members and make sure everyone has understood each new development by, when necessary, making the question into a statement, e.g. 'Yes, Tom has got an artificial leg.' You can prompt the students to ask for more detail about key episodes they have come up with, e.g. 'Find out more about the accident.' At times, ask a member of the class to summarise the story so far or, if necessary, summarise it yourself.

2 When you reach the end, you'll probably find that you have the bare outline of a story. Ask the students to work in pairs and to find a space and retell the story (this might be in the present or the past) and to add details and dialogue.

3 Ask each pair to choose a short scene and simultaneously enact it as two of the characters. This might be Tom and Jessica or one of them with another character from the story. It doesn't matter if two pairs choose the same scene, but ideally there would be scenes from different moments in the story. While they are doing this, note which scene each pair is playing. Allow time for the students to rehearse their scene twice, the second time focusing on body language and emotion.

4 Narrate the story to the whole class, introducing each pair's scene in sequence in order to make a dramatised version of the whole piece. If two pairs have enacted the same scene, it will be interesting to compare the two different interpretations.

5 Ask the class 'Who made up the story?' They might think you did. Let them know that you only said 'Yes' and 'No' and that they did all the creative work. In my experience, students are usually amazed at this. Themes that my students have come up with have ranged from time travel to murder to playing with a pet dog.

Tree Interviews

Level
Elementary to Advanced

Time
20–30 minutes

Language Links
Personal questions

Aim
To practise personal information type interviews in an imaginative way

1 Ask an imaginative student to sit comfortably on a chair with their eyes closed. Explain that he or she is a tree and proceed to 'interview the tree' in a gentle voice:

'Where do you live?'
'What do you like doing?'
'What's your job?'
'Tell me about your best friend.'

Establish with the other students that you may *only* ask questions which are equally appropriate for a person (so *not* 'Have you got any nests in you?' but rather 'Who lives with you?'). Then monitor while the other students proceed with the interview.

2 After this initial interview is over, the students will be eager to 'be trees' so put them in groups of three to five and let the interviews continue, allowing about five minutes per interview.

3 Bring the whole class together to talk about their experience of seeing the world from the point of view of a tree.

Variation
Do the activity with the students as birds.

3

Personalised Drama Activities

Students bring so much with them into the classroom. Their ideas and experiences are our richest resources. Through drama, students can show each other a great deal about themselves in a supportive environment.

- *Personal Experiences* are activities which give students the opportunity to let other class members know about what is important and personal to them, from dreams and sensations to friends and pets, not forgetting phone calls and e-mails.

- *Truth or Lie?* activities make students listen very closely to each other. Who can tell a tall story?

- *Real-life Conversations* are one way of bringing the students' outside relationships alive in the classroom.

- *Giving Talks* is an activity that you can use again and again to build your students' confidence in extended speaking. The topic is open.

Circle Introductions

Level

Elementary to Advanced

Time

40–50 minutes

Language Links

Introducing other people

Aim

To exchange and remember personal information and practise introductions

1 Before splitting the class into two equal-sized groups, check which students know each other best and make sure they join the same group. One group makes a small standing inner circle facing outwards, the other makes an outer standing circle facing a partner from the inner circle. If necessary, join in to make an even number. Explain that pairs facing each other have two minutes to tell each other about themselves and remember as much as possible about each other.

2 After two minutes, remind the students to remember everything they have heard. Tell the outer circle students to move one place to the left (clockwise). The next pairs have 90 seconds to tell each other about their homes and families and try to remember everything. Repeat this rotating procedure until six different student pairs have spoken. Each time, shorten the turn and change the topic, e.g. hobbies, work or studies, favourite food and drinks, beliefs and values, hopes for the future.

3 Ask the outer circle group and the inner circle to move apart and make two separate seated circles. Allot each member of each group a partner from the other group (someone they don't already know well). Tell them to gather as much information as possible about their partner from the students in their own group who spoke to him or her, so that in ten minutes they are ready to introduce their partner to the whole class. Emphasise that it isn't important if there are mistakes – that's part of the fun.

4 If *you* are involved, introduce your partner to the class. Invite that student to correct any information mistakes at the end and to fill in any glaring omissions. Get all the students simultaneously to practise introducing their partners.

5 Each student is introduced to the class and then corrects and clarifies what has been said.

Variation

This is clearly an activity to use at the start of a course, but it can easily be used at a later stage to find out students' views or experiences regarding any topic. For example, in the case of technology, the rounds could be: your favourite gadget, what you use the internet for, your opinion about mobile phones in public places, what problems technology brings us, etc. In this case, ask students just to report back on the most interesting points their allotted partner made.

Close Friends

Level
Elementary to Advanced

Time
25–35 minutes

Language Links
Describing relationships

Aim
To find out about close personal relationships through roleplay

Variation

Of course, any outside relationship can be brought into the room. We can learn a lot about people from their last English teacher, their boss, colleague or employee, family members or even love partners!

1 Introduce yourself to the class as your close friend, e.g. 'Hello, I'm Matt, I'm one of your teacher's (David's) friends. You can ask me about David and my relationship with him.' Answer any questions for about five minutes, revealing as much as you wish. Make a point of diplomatically not answering over-familiar questions, e.g. 'I'd rather not say'. Students will soon realise they are learning a great deal about their teacher.

2 Tell the students to form groups of four or five and take turns to roleplay a close friend (or possibly a relative) being interviewed about their relationship. If necessary, prompt the other students to ask about the friend's relationship with the student in question. The other students will quickly learn a lot about their classmate from their 'close friend'.

My Pet

Level

Elementary to Advanced

Time

20 minutes

Language Links

Describing relationships and pets

Aim

To describe a family pet vividly

1 Elicit usual types of pets and encourage the students to mime holding each one as they practise the pronunciation.

2 Describe one of your pets (if you don't have one, imagine you do – be realistic) and mime holding and, if appropriate, stroking it. Use the prompt questions below to bring it to life. Let another student touch, stroke or even hold it for a moment.

3 Invite the students to guess if your story is true. Then say:

'You're going to describe one of your pets to someone who doesn't know if you really have one. If you don't have a pet, imagine you do. Which pet are you going to describe?'

Check that every student knows the name of their pet species. Ask them to stand with their eyes closed and to imagine their answers to these prompt questions as you slowly and clearly ask them:

- What kind of pet have you brought here today?

- Is it yours?

- What's its name?

- Is it male or female?

- How big is it?

- What does it look like?

- What does it feel like to hold?

- Has it got its own smell?

- How old is it?

- How did you get it?

- What about its character?

- Who does it like best? Why?

- What do you like about it?

- Has it got a bad habit?

- Is there an interesting story you can tell?

4 Ask the students to open their eyes and mime holding their pet. Say:

'Stand with a student who doesn't know if you really have a pet or not. Show them your pet and describe it to them. If it's safe, let your partner touch it. When you've both finished, ask each other questions for more information. Don't say if it's true or not. OK? You've got five minutes.'

As each pair finishes, ask them to hold their partner's pet and quickly show it to another student who has finished.

5 Form a standing circle. Invite each student to say whose pet they're holding and find out if it's a real pet. For example:

Maria: I've got Juan's white cat, Blanca.
Juan: I haven't really got a pet.

Favourite Places

Level
> Lower-intermediate to Advanced

Time
> 20–35 minutes

Language Links
> Describing places

Aim
> To find out about and experience each other's favourite places

1 Ask the students to sit in a circle. Tell them you're going to take them on a journey and ask them to close their eyes. Read slowly, pausing between questions:

'Sit up straight in your chair and close your eyes … Breathe in slowly (let them hear the sound of you breathing in) and breathe out … Breathe in … and out.

Each time you breathe out, breathe out for a little longer … and breathe in slowly. … As you breathe, feel your body relax. … Now you're relaxed. Listen to the sounds outside this room … now listen to the sounds inside this room … now listen to the sound of your breathing. …

Now you're going to your favourite place. … I'm going to ask you some questions. … Please answer them to yourself in your head, but don't speak, keep your eyes closed. … Where are you? … Who are you with? Or are you alone? … Look around. What do you see? … Listen. What can you hear? … What do you smell? … How do you feel? … What are you doing? … You're feeling really happy. Why are you happy? … Now listen to your breathing, listen to the sounds in the classroom, you're back in the classroom … you can open your eyes.'

2 Now provide the students with a model. 'Guide' them round your favourite place, moving across the room and gesturing. Answer their questions as if you are there, e.g. 'I'm on my favourite beach in Hawaii and you're all here with me. Yes, you're right, it *is* hot. Can you feel the sun on your shoulders? I'm sitting on my towel looking at the sea. Look over here! Look at that huge wave crashing onto the beach. It's exciting, isn't it? Let's go surfing, shall we?'

3 Ask the students to stand in groups of three or four and to take turns to guide each other round their favourite place.

Variations

Of course scary or hated places are best left alone, but what about the most exotic place you've ever been, your home, the room where you spend most time or even your fantasy dream place?

My Best Ever Meal

Level
    Lower-intermediate to Advanced

Time
    15–20 minutes

Language Links
    Describing meals

Aim
    To describe the experience of a favourite
    meal in detail

1 Ask the students to sit in circle, hands on knees, eyes closed. Tell them to imagine the answers to your questions. In a calm, clear voice, allowing long pauses, say:

'Relax … breathe in slowly … breathe out slowly … in … out. As you breathe in through your nose, there will be a delicious smell … the smell of the most delicious food you have ever eaten in your life … you can smell it now. … Remember a wonderful meal you had. … Where were you? … When was it? … Who were you with? … Why were you together? … How did you feel? … What did you have as a starter? … Describe it. … What was it made of? … What did it look like? … What did it taste like? … How did it feel in your mouth? … What about the temperature? … What did you drink with it? … What about the next course? … Describe it. … What did you have for dessert? … How was that? … How did you finish the meal? … What did you do after the meal? … In a few moments, you're going to invite another student to enjoy your meal. … When you're ready, open your eyes.'

2 Put the students in pairs, with students who you might expect to have different diets partnering each other. Ask them to sit facing each other. Demonstrate that you would like student A not only to describe their meal but also to roleplay sharing it with B who should ask questions such as, 'Who am I sitting next to?' 'What is this soup made from?' 'Can I use my fingers?' Give the As and then the Bs several minutes to share their best ever meals with their partners before getting whole-class feedback.

Photo Memories

Level Elementary to Advanced **Time** 40–50 minutes **Materials** One blank card (photo-size) per student **Language Links** Describing photos **Aim** To describe and talk about important personal photos

1 Tell the students you have a photo from your childhood in front of you and that you are going to describe it to them in detail, without showing them, so they have to imagine the picture in their mind's eye. Describe a real photo (you must be in it) to them, although you're actually looking at a blank photo-size card, including details prompted by the questions in stage 2 below. On finishing your description, ask the students to picture the photo. Let them ask a few questions about it so that they can imagine it in detail, before revealing to them you have been describing a blank card. Point out that you don't physically need a photo in front of you in order to give a detailed description and that this photo is in fact real although you don't have it with you today.

2 Give each student a blank photo-size card and emphasise to them that it is a *real* photo from their childhood (not made up). Tell them to close their eyes and answer the following questions silently to themselves. Ask the questions clearly, leaving time for the students to think about their answers:

- Who are you with in the photo?
- Where was the picture taken?
- Who took the picture?
- How old were you?
- What were you doing?
- How did you feel?
- Why did you feel like that?
- What were you wearing?
- Why is the photo special for you?

3 Put the students in pairs, A and B, and tell them to hand their 'photo' to each other and take turns to describe their photo to their partner. Tell them to focus on the card, listen to and remember their partner's description while imagining the photo. They can ask questions for clarification.

4 Tell the students to hold on to their partner's 'photo' and make new pairs. They should each 'show' and describe their first partner's photo.

5 Ask the students to make new pairs and to think of a special, more recently-taken photo showing them with one other person. Both students share as much information about the photos as possible in two minutes.

6 Ask the pairs to choose one of the two photos and 'make' the photo, i.e. make a frozen tableau. Stand in the middle and tell them you have the camera so that all the students focus on the centre of room. In turn, each pair 'explains' their frozen tableau to the others, e.g. 'This is my daughter, Ursula. We are riding bicycles on holiday and you can see the farmhouse where we stayed in the background.'

Optional

Repeat stage 6 using the other pair member's photo.

Personal E-mails

Level

Lower-intermediate to Advanced

Time

10 minutes

Language Links

E-mails

Aim

To talk about and find out about personal correspondence

1 Be prepared to talk about a real e-mail or letter you have received from a friend. Stand in front of the students, take out, unfold and look at a piece of paper, without letting the students see that it's blank. Tell them it's a print-out of an e-mail (or a letter) that you received recently. Invite them to ask as many questions as they like, and answer the ones you want to, letting them know in some detail about your relationship with that friend, the purpose of the message and the result. Keep referring to and quoting from the pretend e-mail/letter. 'I'd rather not say' and 'That's private' are useful phrases for them to hear you use before the next stage. Finally, reveal that the paper is blank but that you were talking about a real e-mail or letter.

2 Ask the students to raise their hands if they can think of a personal e-mail or letter they recently received and which they are happy to talk about publicly. Give up to half of the class a blank piece of paper representing their e-mail or letter and pair or group them with the others to answer the questions they want to. After a few minutes, invite feedback.

Variation

In a business context, do the same with a transactional e-mail.

Personal Phone Call

Level Elementary to Advanced **Time** 20–25 minutes **Language Links** Telephoning **Aim** To talk about and practise making telephone calls

1 Ask the students to sit in a circle. Mime holding a phone to your ear and act out a summarised version of one side of an interesting real phone conversation you had recently in about a minute. Be the other person talking to you (not yourself) and make it clear that it's you that you are talking to by using your name (and any appropriate identifying details). After hanging up, ask the class the following questions (simplify them for lower levels):

- Who was the person I was playing?
- What's their relationship to me?
- What was the purpose of the call?
- What was the result?
- How did this person feel?
- How did I feel?
- Do you think this was a real phone call? (Yes, it was!)

2 Ask the students to close their eyes and tell them to think of an interesting real phone call they had recently, which they are happy to talk about in this class. Ask them to think about the answers to these questions:

- Who made the call?
- Who was the other person?
- What's their relationship to you?
- What was the purpose of the call?
- What was the result?
- How did you feel?
- What about the other person?

3 Tell the students to open their eyes and move their chairs so that they are sitting facing a partner. Say:

'Decide who is A and who is B. A, you have one minute to find out as much as you can about B's phone call. OK?'

After a minute, stop the class and say:

'Now you're going to make that call in just two minutes, this time in English. If it was a long call, just do the most important bits. So A, you are B and B, you are the other person you spoke to on the phone. OK? 3-2-1 (make a ringtone sound).'

Stop them after two minutes.

4 Repeat stage 3 with each A working with a new B and re-enacting A's call.

5 Find out from the whole class about the number of different kinds of call that were made, i.e. how many involved friends or family, how many were official, happy, strange, etc. Give a couple of pairs the opportunity to perform an interesting extract for the rest of the class.

Senses

Level

Lower-intermediate to Advanced

Time

15–25 minutes

Language Links

Expressing likes and describing sensations

Aim

To talk about favourite sense experiences

1 Put a DO NOT DISTURB sign outside the room. Ask the students to sit close to a partner and elicit and write up the five senses: hearing, sight, touch, taste and smell.

2 Ask the students to close their eyes and, in a calm voice, give the following instructions (simplify them for lower levels):

'In a couple of minutes, you are going to describe some of your favourite things to your partner. Be aware of your hearing. Imagine you can hear something you love to listen to. What is it? What does it sound like? Is it loud or quiet or does it change? How does it make you feel? Be aware of your eyes. Don't open your eyes, but imagine you can see something you love to look at. What is it? Is it near or far? Dark or bright? What about the shape and the colour? How does it make you feel? Open your hands. Be aware of your palms and your fingertips. Imagine you are touching something you love to touch. What is it? How does it feel? What about the temperature? Be aware of your mouth. Imagine you have in your mouth some food you love to taste. What is it?

What sensations do you feel in your mouth? Be aware of your nose. Imagine you are smelling something you love to smell. What is it? Breathe in through your nose. How does it make you feel? In a moment you're going to talk about the things you imagined. It's OK if you don't want to talk about some of the things. Speak quietly and listen closely to your partner and imagine touching, tasting, smelling, hearing and seeing the same things.'

Here you can sense whether the students need to open their eyes or are relaxed and calm enough to listen to and understand each other with their eyes still closed. Encourage a calm and quiet atmosphere.

3 As each pair finishes, ask them to talk about special memories associated with these sensations until the whole class has finished.

Anecdote Endings

Level
Elementary to Advanced

Time
20–30 minutes

Language Links
Past narrative tenses

Aim
To tell and listen to true anecdotes and guess the endings

1 Tell the students the first part of a short true anecdote about yourself with either a happy or a sad ending. Establish clearly who was involved, where and when it happened and stop at the climax where different endings are possible.

2 Put the students in pairs and give them a minute to bring the story to a happy or unhappy conclusion.

3 Ask them to form new pairs and give them 30 seconds to tell each other their endings. When they have finished, ask them how different their endings are. Ask to hear one happy and one unhappy ending from the whole class before telling them the true ending.

4 Ask the students to think of a short true personal anecdote with a climax and to raise a hand only when they've thought of one. Once a third have an anecdote (As), group them with two students who haven't (B and C). Tell them that the As will tell their anecdote stopping at the climax. The Bs must immediately invent and tell a happy ending and the Cs an unhappy (but possible) ending, both in the first person before the As tell them the real ending.

Optional

Let other groups hear the three different endings of some of the stories and guess which is true and whose story it is.

Impressions

Level

Elementary to Advanced

Time

10–15 minutes

Language Links

Exchanging opinions

Aim

To encourage prediction and active listening

1 Ask the students to sit facing a partner they don't know very well but would like to know better. Ask them to look at each other and think about their answers to the following questions, without showing their answers on their faces:

- What does your partner like about this town/city?

- What is their favourite place in this town/city?

- What don't they like about this town/city? Why?

- What other place would your partner most like to live in? Why? What would they do there?

- Where would your partner like to be living in ten years' time? Why?

2 Tell the pairs to exchange ideas and find out how accurate their guesses were. Do not give them written prompts. It is more natural if they discuss their answers in the order they remember them and sometimes digress.

3 Ask for feedback from the whole class. What was the most interesting thing their partner said about this town?

Variation

Vary the questions to lead in to a new topic and encourage students to listen actively to each other.

Dreams and Fantasies

Level
   Lower-intermediate to Advanced

Time
   10–20 minutes

Language Links
   Present narrative tenses

Aim
   To practise telling and bringing to life
   personal dreams and fantasies

---

1 Ask the students to sit in a circle. Tell and bring to
life with some gesture and mime a dream or
fantasy that you've had. Invite questions and
comments about the possible meaning before
revealing if you have really had that
dream/fantasy or made it up (ideally you will
choose a real one).

2 Ask the students to raise a hand if they have had
a dream or fantasy they are happy to talk about.
Once half the students have their hands raised,
pair them with the remaining students (if fewer
than half, make groups). Give the dream/fantasy
students three minutes to tell (and, if willing,
bring to life with gesture and mime) their dream
or fantasy and answer their partner's questions
about it so that their partner knows enough to tell
the whole class.

3 Ask for a few volunteers to tell their partner's
dream/fantasy. If they are willing, the original
dreamer/fantasiser can simultaneously act out
through mime their role in it.

4 If appropriate, ask for interpretations from the
other class members before finding out if it was
made up or not.

Lost and Found

Level
   Elementary to Advanced

Time
   15 minutes

Language Links
   Past narrative tenses

Aim
   To practise telling and bringing to life
   personal anecdotes

1 Ask the students to sit in a circle. Mime handing
an object you once lost and found to a student.
Tell the whole class a short true anecdote,
accompanied by mime and gesture, about the
time you lost and then found this thing (use the
prompt questions below as a guide).

2 Tell the students to close their eyes and say:

'Remember a time when you lost and then found
something. ... If you don't have a story in your
head, you can make one up. Think about your
answers to the following questions. Where were
you? ... When? ... Who were you with? ... What
did you lose? ... How did you feel about this
thing? ... How did you lose it? ... When did you
realise you'd lost it? ... How did you react? ...
How did you feel? ... What did you do next? ...
How did you find it again? ... How did you feel

when you found it? ... How do you feel when you
remember this story? ... Now open your eyes.
You're going to stand with a partner and let them
give you the thing they once lost. Find out about
their story and remember it. Don't say if it's a true
story or not. OK? Stand with your partner. Decide
who is going to tell their story first. You've got
three minutes.'

Make sure the student telling their story mimes
giving the thing they lost to their partner.

3 After three minutes, encourage the pairs to
change over roles of teller and listener. When
everyone has finished, ask them all to stand in a
circle, 'holding' the thing their partner lost and
found. If time allows, quickly find out what they
are holding and if they think it's a true story
before checking with their partner.

Spot the Lie

Level
   Elementary to Advanced

Time
   10–15 minutes

Language Links
   Speculating

Aim
   To focus on active listening and speaking personally

1 Talk about yourself for two minutes, either on a topic you are currently studying or on a subject selected by the students, e.g. your hobbies, allowing the students to ask for further information. Afterwards let them know that one thing you said was untrue. Invite pairs of students to speculate about what they think the lie could be before you elicit their guesses and finally reveal the lie (and the truth!).

2 Put the students in groups of three or four, ideally with the classmates they know the least well, to play the game. Use the same subject or elicit and write up a selection of topics which they can choose from.

NOTE: This is an effective way of introducing or reviewing a topic.

Liar

<table>
<tr><td>

Level

Lower-intermediate to Advanced

Time

25 minutes

Language Links

Further-information questions

Aim

To convince others that a false story is true

</td></tr>
</table>

NOTE: This activity requires a minimum of six students and a maximum of 15.

Preparation

At some point before the lesson, arrange a quick secret meeting with a student to find out an interesting and unusual personal fact which none of the other class members know about and which could, in theory, be true for anyone in the class, e.g. 'I broke my big toe at the swimming pool when I was ten' or 'One of my relatives can read hieroglyphics'. Make sure the student knows they have to keep the meeting secret from the rest of the class.

1 Write on the board and announce the fact to the class as if it's true of *yourself*; tell them some made-up details to make it plausible. At this stage, it might be a good idea to write up and present a few items of essential vocabulary which the students can use later. Invite questions and answer them. After a couple of minutes, reveal that this fact is not true for you but it is true for one of them.

2 Immediately, ask them all to close their eyes and tell them that they are going to make the other students believe that the fact is actually true about them. They are all liars except for one. Ask them questions, which they can answer to themselves in silence, to help them embellish the details of their story. These questions should be about time, place, people involved, feelings, results, etc. (the questions will depend to some degree on the nature of the fact in question). For example:

'What time of year was it when you broke your big toe? What kind of swimming pool was it? You'll need to describe it ...'

Explain to the students that they will not find out who is telling the truth until the very end of the activity. Also explain that they must be careful not to contradict themselves when talking to different students, or they are sure to be found out.

3 Ask the students to open their eyes, stand up and spend five minutes moving from person to person, quizzing each other about their stories.

4 At the end of the five minutes, form a standing circle and give each student the opportunity to say the name of one student they definitely think is lying. The student with the most votes sits down. Even if they are the one telling the truth, they must not reveal this. Continue this process of voting until there are just five students remaining on their feet. These five have up to a minute each to tell their story to the whole class. Two more students are then voted out by those already eliminated.

Liar

5 Form three equal-sized groups. Each group has two minutes with each of the three remaining students to interrogate them before the next student is voted out.

6 Finally, the two remaining students face each other and have 30 seconds each to say why their opponent is a liar, starting 'You are a liar because …' The last student is voted out. Before revealing if the students have found the truth-teller, go round all the students asking them if they were in fact telling the truth. Of course you should not reveal the identity of the truth-teller until the very end.

Exaggeration

Level
Elementary to Advanced

Time
15–20 minutes

Language Links
Exaggerating

Aim
To experiment with exaggerating when recounting anecdotes

---

1 Discuss with the students the fact that many people enjoy exaggerating the truth.

2 Tell them to listen to you recounting a true anecdote and to challenge anything they think may be untrue. Make sure you use exaggerated stress and intonation on the untrue parts, e.g.

You: Last Wednesday after school I drove to my dentist in *London*.

Students: Your dentist can't be so far away.

You: Oh, you're right. She's on the other side of Exeter. So anyway I had to wait at least *three hours* to see her ...

3 Give the students a few moments to think of a suitable true anecdote they can tell before putting them in groups of three or four to listen to and challenge each other's exaggerated stories.

Last Night's Chat

Level

Elementary to Advanced

Time

15–20 minutes

Language Links

Reporting conversations

Aim

To discuss, report and roleplay personal conversations

1 Form a standing circle. Approach a few students, making the same true statement using this formula:

'At home last night I chatted to my ... about ...'

2 Give the students two minutes to circulate and do the same, remembering who each of the others chatted to last night and what the conversation was about.

3 Reform the circle. Refer to a student, saying, for example: 'At home last night *Sophie* chatted to her *landlady* about ...' gesturing to the other students that they should all say the topic of conversation, e.g. 'learning French'. The named student then continues by referring to another group member and the whole group says their topic of conversation and so on.

4 Put the students in pairs, A and B. Tell the As they have one minute to tell the Bs more about their own chat from last night. Then give A and B two minutes to roleplay part of the conversation (in English!) as truthfully or imaginatively as they wish. When they have finished, reverse the process so the focus is now on B's chat from last night.

5 Ask each pair to choose one of the two conversations and, in turn, to show an extract to the others. After observing, the other students name the conversation partner and the conversation topic, e.g. 'Jon is playing Sophie talking to her landlady (played by Sophie) about learning French.' Recalling stage 3 will help them.

Don't Drink the Water

Level

    Elementary to Advanced

Time

    15–20 minutes

Language Links

    Advice and warnings

Aim

    To practise and discuss giving advice
    and warnings

Variations

Advice/warnings could be about studying a particular subject, doing their job, training for a sport, going out on the town, living away from home, etc.

1 If the students are studying in an English-speaking country, find out one person who gave each of them the most advice and/or warnings before they came, perhaps a family member or a friend. If the students are not studying in an English-speaking country, ask them to say who would give them advice or warnings in that situation. Brainstorm and write up the subject matter of the advice, e.g. carrying money, staying out late, crossing the road, etc.

2 Put the students in pairs, A and B, and give them a minute each to find out as much as they can about what advice and warnings that person gave or would give their partner.

3 Ask A to roleplay the person warning or advising A while B pretends to be A, responding to the advice or warnings. After a few minutes, ask them to exchange roles.

4 Ask for whole-class feedback on the most interesting and humorous examples.

Quick Personal Talks

Level
> Elementary to Advanced

Time
> 15–20 minutes

Language Links
> Connecting ideas

Aim
> To develop fluency by talking personally

Variation

Use this activity often as a lead-in or follow-up to find out quickly about the students' personal experience of any topic you are covering, e.g. their work, specialist area of study, hobby, diet, etc. Students will do it more successfully each time and get a big confidence boost from the extended speaking involved.

1 Invite the students to ask you as many questions as possible in one minute about being a teacher. After the minute is up, immediately give a two-minute talk on the subject of 'My life as a teacher', incorporating answers to some, but not all, of the questions. After finishing, point out that you only chose the questions you wanted to answer and that you didn't answer the questions as a list but integrated the answers into a talk. You can also admit that you quite naturally forgot some of the questions.

2 Elicit and write up some topics for students to give a talk about, e.g. my last holiday, my hobby, etc.

3 Put the students in groups of three, A, B and C. Tell A to choose a topic and B and C to ask questions for one minute. Then tell A to give a two-minute talk.

4 Repeat the process for B and C.

4

Conversation Skills

Learners of English can benefit a great deal from exploring what are regarded as 'good conversation skills' in English. In the activities in this section, students have the chance to look at isolated elements of communication and try them out. They can then discuss cultural and language similarities and differences between the English spoken in Western English-speaking countries, International English and their own mother tongue. These activities are suitable for learners from all language and cultural backgrounds.

If you are planning to use several of these activities during a course, I would recommend doing them in a similar order to that in which they appear here. It makes sense to look at the most fundamental skills, like *showing interest*, early on.

Greetings

Level
Elementary to Advanced

Time
35 minutes

Language Links
Greetings

Aim
To greet other English speakers appropriately

1 Ask the students to estimate the following:

- How many times they've talked to another person in the last week.
- Whether they started more or less than 50 per cent of these exchanges.
- What percentage were with strangers.

2 Elicit the types of people they have talked to and write them on the board in the following categories:

Informal	**Semi-formal**
Friends	Teachers
Classmates	Colleagues
Younger family members	Older family members
	New students
Formal	Friends of friends
Older strangers	

3 Ask the students to stand in as big a circle as possible. Tell them you are going to start talking to them in turn and in each case all the students should listen and decide what the relationships might be and the situation. Move from one student to another quickly, using the following greetings with natural and friendly intonation:

- 'Excuse me, is anyone sitting here?' F
- 'Pleased to meet you, my name's … .' F

- 'Hello, how are you today?' S F
- 'Hi, (name)! How are things?' I
- 'Terrible weather, isn't it?' I
- 'Oh, hello! Nice to see you here.' S F
- 'All right? You look really tired.' I

4 Ask the students to recall the greetings you used and to tell you where to write them up next to the list in stage 2. Discuss possible situations. Then tell the students to practise all the exponents, focusing on lively intonation.

5 Ask each student to come up and greet you in turn, using the above exponents; tell them all to focus on your responses. Respond briefly as naturally as possible, always positively.

6 Now the students are ready to practise. Get them all walking round the room randomly in different directions, focusing on not touching each other and avoiding eye contact. Tell them that when you call out a greeting situation they should look for a partner, make eye contact, smile and start a natural conversation. Each time, stop the conversation after 20 seconds and get them walking round again before calling out the next greeting situation. You could call out this sequence:

- Good friends in the pub
- Meeting your new colleague for the first time
- Strangers waiting for a bus
- Classmates before the lesson
- Strangers in a busy café
- A friend of a friend at a party (you can't remember their name!)
- Your teacher, who wasn't very well yesterday

7 As a class, discuss the importance of confidence, lively intonation and body language when starting a conversation.

Showing Interest

Level
Elementary to Advanced

Time
30 minutes

Language Links
Showing interest

Aim
To respond appropriately in conversations by showing interest in what others say

1 Ask the students (if they have had the experience) how they find keeping conversations going in English with native speakers. Ask them how you can show people you're interested in what they're saying. Elicit things such as body language, facial expressions, intonation, non-verbal utterances, verbal prompts.

Write the following on the board:

SHOWING INTEREST	
Body language	**Facial expression**
open posture	eye contact
leaning forward	raising eyebrows
nodding	smiling
AGREEMENT/UNDERSTANDING: intonation	
Non-verbal	**Verbal**
mm	yes/yeah
uh-huh	right / all right
	OK
	sure
	fine
SURPRISE: intonation	
Non-verbal	**Verbal**
mm	oh
ah	really
	right

2 Get the students to practise 'agreement' and 'surprise' intonation, using the different exponents above.

3 Sit the students in pairs, A and B, facing each other. Tell A to talk about his or her free time while B shows *zero* interest. i.e. no eye contact, arms, legs folded, etc. After a few moments, tell A and B to swap roles.

4 Elicit reactions from the whole class. Students may suggest words like 'uncomfortable' or 'horrible'.

5 Now ask A to talk while B *exaggerates* showing interest (unless students make a joke of it, the exaggerated version will probably sound and feel much more positive). Get the students to swap roles after a few minutes.

6 Ask the students to work in groups of three and to talk about studying English, encouraging them to 'show interest' when other students are talking. Alternatively, if you feel it is appropriate for your class to study this in more detail, ask B to show interest in what A says while C observes what B does to show interest. After a minute, C and A give B feedback. Repeat this twice so that each group member has a turn as talker, listener and observer.

7 As a whole class, discuss the differences and similarities between the language, both physical and oral, used to show interest by native English speakers and that used in the students' own mother tongue.

Information Questions

Level

Elementary to Advanced

Time

20–25 minutes

Language Links

Requesting information

Aim

To ask information questions to maintain conversation

1 Elicit from the students that an effective way of keeping a conversation going is to ask questions for further information as *everyone* loves talking about themselves. Point out that many of these questions are often shortened. Elicit and write the following questions on the board (along with any other short questions offered by the class):

1 Who with?
2 Why?
3 Where?
4 What about?
5 What time?
6 Which one?
7 How long?
8 How much?

2 Read out the following story (or something similar) as naturally as possible, allowing the students to ask questions from the board until they get the right one for you to continue (the number refers to the question above):

'I went out last night … (1) With Jan. We went to see Casablanca at the cinema … (6) The Picture House. The tickets were rather expensive … (8) £8.80 each! Anyway we got there really early … (5) About 7.30. We didn't want to miss the start. But we still had to queue for ages … (7) It seemed like at least 30 minutes … (2) Because lots of people had booked in advance and it wasn't clear if there would be any seats left. Anyway we got the worst seats possible … (3) Right in the front row near the screen. I had to walk out after ten minutes, so I complained to the manager … (4) It was too noisy and I couldn't focus my eyes on the screen, we were so close …'

3 Put the students in groups of three to five. Invite the most confident member of each group to start telling the others about a recent evening when they went out while the others ask as many short questions as possible. Even though they may ask more short questions than is natural, it is important to get familiar with using them. After the first student finishes, each of the others has a turn.

4 As a whole class, discuss the importance of questions in maintaining conversations, and any cultural differences (personal questions are regarded as being more intrusive in some cultures than in others).

Expressing Common Experience

Level
Lower-intermediate to Advanced

Time
30–40 minutes

Language Links
Exchanging personal information

Aim
To express common experience in order to develop conversation skills

1 Draw a picture of a tree in winter.

Discuss with the students how, when a conversation starts, we don't usually know where it will end – there are an infinite number of places it can branch off. Ask them if they have ever traced a conversation backwards to see how one idea linked to another (use the tree picture to illustrate). Point out that what one person says may trigger an idea in another person's mind because of common experience.

2 Ask a student to tell you what he or she did last night. At an appropriate moment, respond with the 'common experience' phrase in stage 3 below, using lively intonation. Make sure that you repeat the phrase the student uses which 'triggers' your interjection. For example:

Masako: I had a cheese and tomato pizza for dinner last night.

You: Really? That's amazing. You had cheese? I bought a cheese sandwich for my lunch earlier …

3 Write the following on the board and get the students to practise, focusing on intonation and substituting the different adjectives.

EXPRESSING COMMON EXPERIENCE		
Really? That's	interesting funny/strange amazing/incredible	(Repeat, explain)
e.g. Really? That's interesting. You fell asleep on the sofa? I was really tired last night too …		

4 Tell the students that they are going to start a conversation on the subject of trees and that they should take over from each other by expressing common experience. Before starting, brainstorm verbs and verb phrases that can have 'tree' as their object and write them up around the tree picture. For example:

to plant, to have, to crash into, to sit under, to grow, to see, to bump into, to have a picnic under, to cut back, to climb, to dance round, to cut down, to fall out of, to touch, etc.

5 Put the students in groups of three to five and tell them to have conversations about trees. After a few minutes, stop them and discuss how some people are much more likely to interrupt and take over the conversation than others, and that in most English-speaking countries this is perfectly polite and friendly and makes conversation lively and interesting. Encourage the students to have a new conversation in their group, this time allowing complete freedom regarding subject matter and direction. Tell them the conversation may 'branch off' in any direction, so they must listen carefully.

6 After five to ten minutes, ask the students to backtrack and recall the points where one idea sparked off a new direction in the conversation. Suggest they practise these conversation skills in future English conversations.

Exchanging Personal Information

Level

Lower-intermediate to Advanced

Time

20–25 minutes

Language Links

Exchanging personal information

Aim

To practise giving and receiving personal information in the context of personal relationships

1 Invite a confident student to come to the front and ask you what you did last night. Answer, giving away minimal detail, e.g. 'I went to the cinema'. Invite the same student to ask you again and this time give a full answer (but not too much information!) using lively intonation, e.g. 'I went to see *The Rocky Horror Show* with my friend Steve last night. It was really brilliant, but so noisy …' Ask the student which of the two answers makes it easier to continue the conversation. Ask what he or she did last night. Show interest and encourage further details without using questions, e.g. 'It must have been very busy in that bar' or 'Yes, and it was raining really hard'. Then find a good moment to share some personal information about yourself connected to what they say. For example, if he or she talks about last night's takeaway, you might respond 'Oh, I didn't have a takeaway, but I wish I had. The curry I made didn't have much taste at all.'

2 Tell the students that psychologists have shown that Reciprocal Self-disclosure (receiving and giving personal information in turn) helps to build and strengthen personal relationships, but only if it is a two-way process. Point out that most conversations are not actually a series of questions and anwers. Elicit and write up a list of four or five suitable topics and ask the students to sit with a partner that they would like to know more about and spend five minutes receiving and giving information on one of the topics. Ask them not to use questions but to show interest and make sure the amount of information each of them gives is more-or-less equal.

3 Invite feedback and comments before asking the students to change partners and topics. Each time they change partners, remind them to disclose as much information as their partner does (and not just solicit information).

Hesitating

Level

Lower-intermediate to Advanced

Time

25–30 minutes

Language Links

Hesitating

Aim

To promote long-turn speaking; to use English hesitation devices naturally in conversation

1 Find out from the students if, when they're speaking their native language, they sometimes can't find the words to express what they want to say. Tell them that you're going to speak unprepared for a couple of minutes on any topic the students give you. Tell them to listen actively and remember what you do when you are looking for the words you need.

While you speak, use and slightly emphasise the hesitation utterances listed below:

um …
er …
well …
let me see …
I mean …
you know …
you know what I mean …
the thing is …
sort of …
kind of …
you see …
what was it?

2 Elicit and write on the board the above hesitation utterances and practise the pronunciation. Point out that in a conversation we use these utterances, as well as body language, to stop the other person from taking over because we haven't finished what we want to say (our 'turn'). If appropriate, demonstrate this with a confident student, talking on the same topic as in stage 1.

3 Elicit and write up at least five more suitable conversation topics. Tell the students they need to use as many different hesitation utterances as possible in a two-minute conversation with a partner. They must use them to prevent their partner interrupting and must count how many different ones their partner uses and note what they are. Once the students are standing in pairs, announce the topic of the first two-minute conversation, choosing the easiest one from the list. After two minutes, each student tells their partner how many different hesitation utterances he or she used and which ones. Encourage the students to use different utterances in their next conversation.

4 Tell the students to change partners and announce a new topic. Repeat the same procedure several times.

Interpersonal Distances

Level
Lower-intermediate to Advanced

Time
20–25 minutes

Language Links
Formal and informal conversation

Aim
To explore how interpersonal distances are related to conversation

1 Clear an open space and put the students in groups of three, A, B and C. (If necessary, have one or two pairs.) Tell them it's late in the evening and they're in a quiet city street. Ask A to stand with his or her back to the wall so it is impossible to move backwards. Tell B and C that they are police officers and ask them to stand facing A, two metres away. Explain to B and C that someone saw A at 9 p.m. last night near the street where a car was broken into. They are going to interview A for five minutes to check his or her story. Before starting, tell them not to move from where they are standing.

2 After two minutes tell B and C to take one big step towards A so that they are about 1 metre away and after another two minutes, tell B and C to move forward so that they are shoulder to shoulder about 40 cm away from and face to face with A. Stop the interview after a short time when the students find it difficult to continue.

3 Ask A to tell B and C how it felt when they came close and ask B and C to tell A what they noticed about A's body language. Then invite whole-class feedback. Explain that studies show that even innocent people show signs of evasiveness such

as breaking eye contact and putting their arms up in front of them when a police officer questions them at too close a distance.

4 Explain to the class that psychologists define four interpersonal distances (the measurements below refer to research in the UK and North America):

Intimate distances: 15–45cm
Personal distances: 45–120cm
Social distances: 120–210cm
Public distances: 360–600cm

5 Put the students in pairs, A and B, and ask them to stand in a frozen position as if they were close friends talking about their weekend plans and to note the distance (personal) before bringing the scene to life.

6 After a minute do the same with the students as car salesperson and customer (social), then as a loving couple saying how they feel about each other or, if this is too awkward for your class, perhaps a parent comforting an upset child (intimate). Finally, ask a confident student to stand at the front and be a tour guide showing a group of tourists (the others) around an important historic building (public).

7 Elicit situations where the different distances are most appropriate. For example:

Intimate: comforting, protecting, crowding, fighting
Personal: close friends and family
Social: typical of business and professional/client relationships
Public: public speaking where it is not necessary for listeners to respond

8 Ask the students to compare interpersonal distances in their countries with those typical of the UK and North America (given above).

Closing a Conversation

Level
Lower-intermediate to Advanced

Time
20 minutes

Language Links
Saying goodbye

Aim
To explore the conventions of closing conversations

1 Form a seated circle. Turn towards a student sitting next to you and start talking about a topic of interest, e.g. the last thing they bought. Show a lot of interest but suddenly break off while they are talking, stand up and walk away saying 'Bye' over your shoulder. Acknowledge the rudeness of your abrupt departure and apologise to the student. Establish that there are often three stages in closing a conversation among native speakers in most English-speaking countries. Write these three headings on the board:

- Finishing the conversation
- Statement about a different topic (e.g. the future)
- Final closing expression

2 Ask the same student to talk to you on the same topic again (if they're willing). This time go through the conventions above and use body language (see below) in a slightly exaggerated way. After you've walked away, acknowledge that your performance was a little exaggerated and elicit, write up and practise examples of suitable exponents for the above stages, including:

Finishing the conversation:
Well, (name), it's been great talking to you.
That's really interesting. Thanks, (name).

Statement about a different topic (e.g. future):
Don't be late again tomorrow.
Good luck with the rest of your project.

Final closing expressions:
Bye/Good bye.
Cheerio/Cheers.
See you soon/later/Monday.

3 Elicit, write up and practise body language used (often in the sequence below) by native speakers of English to show that a conversation is coming to a close:

- Extended gaze
- Change in posture
- Explosive hand contacts (if seated, on thigh, desk, etc.)
- Standing up (if seated)
- Increase in interpersonal distance
- Breaking eye contact
- Moving towards an exit

4 Invite comments on whether and how these non-verbal markers are the same or different in the students' own culture (students from some countries don't always pick up on the above markers, which sometimes makes it difficult for a British teacher to close a conversation!).

5 Run through the exponents and body language above once again with the students copying and repeating after you. Then ask pairs simultaneously to act out the last minute of a conversation about their English studies from sitting to standing to leave-taking. While students are doing the pairwork, give them time warnings, e.g. '20 seconds to go', 'five seconds to go'. Once they have finished, refer the pairs back to the verbal and non-verbal markers and ask them to tell their partner which ones they noticed them use.

professional
perspectives

professional perspectives is a series of practical methodology books
designed to provide teachers of English with fresh insights,
innovative ideas and original classroom materials.

Other titles in the series include:

Creating Conversation in Class

by Chris Sion
More than 100 imaginative ideas and stimulating
activities designed to get students talking in class

Talking Business in Class

by Chris Sion
More than 50 engaging activities to provide free-stage
conversation in professional classes

Humanising your Coursebook

by Mario Rinvolucri
A wide range of activities designed to extend typical
coursebook language practice by engaging students
creatively and productively

The MINIMAX Teacher

by Jon Taylor
Practical, easy-to-use activities that generate the
maximum student output from the minimum teacher
input

Using the Mother Tongue

by Sheelagh Deller and Mario Rinvolucri
Ready-to-use activities which make creative use of
the students' mother tongue in the language learning
classroom

Unlocking Self-expression through NLP

by Judith Baker and Mario Rinvolucri
Over 100 speaking activities which draw on the
insights into communication provided by
Neuro-Linguistic Programming

The *Resourceful* English Teacher

by Jonathan Chandler and Mark Stone
A complete teaching companion containing 200
classroom activities for use in a wide range of
teaching situations

For a full list and further details of titles
in the *professional perspectives* series,
contact the publishers at:

DELTA PUBLISHING
39 Alexandra Road
Addlestone
Surrey KT15 2PQ

Tel +44 (0)1932 854776
Fax +44 (0)1932 849528
E-mail info@deltapublishing.co.uk
Web www.deltapublishing.co.uk